# FINDING THE

# RIGHT

## STRATEGY

How to Grow Sales in a

Title Insurance Company


By


Christopher R. Hanson, Ph.D.

and

Roger C. Lubeck, Ph.D.


Corporate Behavior Analysts, Ltd.

It Is What It Is Press

*Happy Holidays*
*Marianne Mathieu*
*Fidelity National Title Group*
*December 2014*

# FINDING THE RIGHT STRATEGY
How to Grow Sales in a Title Insurance Company

Library of Congress
Cataloging-in-Publication Data Available
LCCN 2014908636
It Is What It Is Press, Sugar Grove, Illinois

ISBN-10:0983728186
ISBN-13:978-0-9837281-8-4
283 pages – Revised 9/23/2014

Cover Design by Roger Lubeck and Ted Stanaszek
Photo from iStock_000002984671

It Is What It Is Press
299 S. Foothill Blvd.
Cloverdale, California, 95425
iwiipress.com

# FINDING THE

# RIGHT

## STRATEGY

### How to Grow Sales in a

#### Title Insurance Company

As a follow-up to *Finding the Right Path: A Guide To Leading And Managing A Title Insurance Company*, Chris Hanson and Roger Lubeck from Corporate Behavior Analysts, Ltd., share insights and experiences on the changing nature of sales in the title insurance industry in their new book *Finding the Right Strategy: How To Grow Sales in a Title Insurance Company*.

*Finding the Right Strategy* is based on the authors 23 years of consulting experience. It includes time-tested concepts as well as new sales ideas for the evolving digital age. Title industry executives, agency owners and managers, sales managers and account representatives will discover in *Finding the Right Strategy*, practical ideas and guidelines for the development of sales strategies and tactics.

*Finding the Right Strategy* includes chapters on branding, customer service, determining what customers' value, measuring customer satisfaction, sales skills, creating a sales plan, sales management, and marketing and sales strategies in the digital age.

# Working with
# Corporate Behavior Analysts, Ltd.

"Working with CBA has been an invaluable experience for me and our company. In following the concepts and strategies developed by CBA, we have taken our sales program to another level and will continue to build on that success through our partnership with CBA." Debbie Collins, Vice President, Director of Sales, Meridian Title Corporation, Carmel, Indiana.

"*University* Title Company's success today is because of practices and vision learned from working with CBA." Celia Goode-Haddock, Chairman of the Board/CEO of University Title Company, College Station, Texas.

"Engaging CBA was a turning point for Prairie Title. Roger and Chris do not come into an organization with bold promises to fix it. Instead, they teach their clients how they should think about running their businesses." Frank Pellegrini. CEO. Prairie Title, Oak Park, Illinois.

"The workshops and programs presented by CBA throughout the country have helped hundreds of independent agents meet the challenges brought about by the dynamic changes facing the title industry. Many agents consider CBA to be their 'silent partner!'" George 'Mike' Ramsey, retired in December of 2010 after 44 years in the title industry. He was a Regional Vice President and Agency Manager for Chicago and Fidelity National Title.

"With CBA's fresh set of eyes and patience we were able to develop a plan to navigate through the most difficult business climate our industry has ever experienced. Working with them has not only been productive and enlightening, it has also been enjoyable, which helped make the entire process even more successful." Mark Myers, President, Meridian Title Company, South Bend, Indiana.

## CORPORATE BEHAVIOR ANALYSTS, Ltd.

Corporate Behavior Analysts, Ltd. (CBA) is a Chicago and California based consulting firm providing leadership and management development. Founded in 1997 by Chris Hanson and Roger Lubeck, CBA has worked with hundreds of independent title insurance agents, the two largest title insurance underwriters, and numerous Land Title Associations. As national speakers, authors, and experts on leading and managing title insurance companies, Roger and Chris have consulted with companies in more than thirty states in their journey to find the right paths and strategies for success.

## CHRISTOPHER R. HANSON, Ph.D.

Chris Hanson, Ph.D. is Executive Vice President of CBA. Chris holds degrees in Behavioral Systems Analysis and Clinical Psychology from West Virginia University. He has over 33 years of consulting experience in the public and private sectors. Chris has consulted with early childhood programs throughout the U.S., including establishing integrated services for HIV infected children and their families. Since 1991, Chris has advised and coached business executives and managers in the title industry. In 2011, he co-authored with his business partner Roger Lubeck, *Finding the Right Path: A Guide to Leading and Managing A Title Insurance Company*. Chris is an avid backcountry skier, loves B&W photography, has two daughters, Lindsay and Kristan, and lives with his wife Cheriann in Chicago.

## ROGER C. LUBECK, Ph.D.

Roger Lubeck, Ph.D., is President of Corporate Behavior Analysts, Ltd, and has over 30 years of consulting experience in real estate services, healthcare, higher education, manufacturing, and mental health. Roger has a Ph.D. in Experimental Psychology from Utah State University and degrees in Behavioral Psychology from Western Michigan University. In his career, Roger has been a business consultant, workshop leader, retreat facilitator, public speaker, speechwriter, assistant professor, researcher, parent trainer, and dog catcher. Roger is married to Lynette Chandler, a Professor of Special Education and author. Roger is the author of four published novels and a number of publications on customer service, leadership, management, marketing, and sales.

# DEDICATION

**Christopher R. Hanson**. To Sig Hanson, who provided the foundation and Dorothy Hanson Brown, whose strength provides inspiration.

**Roger Clarke Lubeck**. My middle name is Clarke. The Clarke's came to the United States from Crewkerne in Somerset England. The men in the family were ministers, saddle makers, tycoons, and drunks. Most of all, the men were salespersons. My Grandfather Carl C. Clarke was a great salesperson. This book is dedicated to his spirit.

# PREFACE

Roger and I were trained as psychologists. Although we were not trained as sales people as such, we have practiced consultative selling for many years and believe that customer relationships and ultimately sales are often driven by first understanding what customers value and then delivering services based on that premise. For us, understanding human behavior is an important part of sales. If we look close enough, we find remnants of sales in our collective DNA. My dad owned a business that had him plan interiors for residential homes. Most people would have called him an interior decorator, but he had to develop relationships and trust with his customers, just like any good sales person, long before they would ever let him help choose their home furnishings and commit to actual sales. Roger's grandfather took a Dale Carnegie course on public speaking in the 1930's. By all reports, he was a great salesman.

As we look to the future, we know value-added selling concepts will continue to be a critical component in marketing and sales. This book is our way of sharing our experience and the experiences of others. To that end, we asked a few colleagues to tell us their ideas about sales. We want to thank Terry Brown, Debbie Collins, Celia Goode-Haddock, Ken Lingenfelter, Mark Myers, Frank Pellegrini, George 'Mike' Ramsey, Jack Rattikin III, and John Rogers for their contributions to the book. We have learned much more from them than they likely did from us and we are privileged to pass on their collective wisdom along with a few of our own ideas.

Chris R. Hanson, Ph.D.

ix

# INTRODUCTION

This is the second book in a series. The first book, *Finding the Right Path*, focused on leadership and management of title insurance companies. This book focuses on marketing and sales strategies for title insurance companies. It is a guide for title company owners, executive and management staff, sales managers, and sales staff. As with our first book, this second volume does not cover every topic found in a textbook about strategy or marketing and sales. Rather, it focuses on our experience of over twenty years working in the title industry throughout the country with hundreds of talented management and sales professionals.

This book was written so that each chapter stands on its own, nonetheless, the book could be read chapter by chapter because there is a logical order to the content. The book was written for title industry professionals with examples from title agencies. Nevertheless, there are basic marketing and sales ideas in the book that would be applicable in most businesses.

At the end of each chapter, we present Guiding Principles and Development Ideas and Questions. The Guiding Principles are a summary of the key concepts covered in the chapter. The Development Ideas\Questions section was designed to be used by management and sales teams as a study guide.

*Finding the Right Strategy* starts with an examination of sales and marketing in the title industry. In Chapter 1, we consider differences between sales and marketing, and in Chapter 2, we review the main business strategies that have been in play in the industry for several years. In Chapter 3, we look at branding as a marketing strategy and provide insights on ways you can improve your brand. In Chapters 4, 5, and 6, we study the importance of customer service as one of the few strategies title companies can still compete on and we outline specific actions title companies can take to elevate service above the competition.

We believe the most direct way to determine what customers' value is to ask them. In Chapter 7, we discuss and outline the 12 steps you can follow to interview customers and learn what they need. We are convinced marketing and sales strategies should be built on a solid foundation of understanding what customers' value, want and need.

In Chapter 8, we focus on the mechanics of determining customer satisfaction. The reason, we believe that feedback from customers about a title companies' products and services should be part of the formula that guides future strategic actions.

In Chapters 9 and 10 we look into the sales person's toolbox, identify, and discuss sales skills and sales planning techniques we have seen prove successful. Routinely, we have found that many smaller title companies do not have formal sales plans. It is our opinion, taking the time and making the effort to develop a formal written sales plan is an important operational strategy to grow sales and is within the reach of any title company, even the smallest.

Chapter 11 outlines how to develop the content for a sales plan and follow-through to implement sales strategies and tactics on a consistent basis throughout the year.

Many people think selling is an art, but we know that sales management is not. In Chapter 12, we discuss the components of good sales management.

In the final two chapters, we look toward the future. In Chapter 13, we examine the future of digital sales and the effects the internet and electronic commerce is having and will have on the title industry. We also examine the growing role and influence the consumer will have on strategy selection for title companies in the years ahead. Finally, in Chapter 14, we turn our attention to what you can do to select the right strategies and a path for your title company, as you look to the future.

Collectively, the chapters in this book provide tested ideas that will help you find the right strategies to grow sales in your title company.

# TABLE OF CONTENTS

| | | |
|---|---|---|
| 1. | THE TITLE INDUSTRY | 1 |
| 2. | BUSINESS STRATEGIES | 15 |
| 3. | BRANDING | 25 |
| 4. | CUSTOMER SERVICE | 49 |
| 5. | WOWING CUSTOMERS | 69 |
| 6. | CUSTOMER FOCUS | 83 |
| 7. | CUSTOMER INTERVIEWS | 97 |
| 8. | CUSTOMER SATISFACTION | 117 |
| 9. | SALES SKILLS | 135 |
| 10. | SALES CALLS | 159 |
| 11. | CREATING A SALES PLAN | 169 |
| 12. | MANAGING SALES | 205 |
| 13. | SALES IN THE DIGITAL AGE | 227 |
| 14. | SELECTING A STRATEGY | 241 |

# FINDING THE

# RIGHT

## STRATEGY

How to Grow Sales in a

Title Insurance Company

# THE TITLE INDUSTRY
## CHAPTER 1

This book is about strategies and tactics used to grow sales, to increase revenue and market share. The topics and tips provided in this book will apply to any business, however, we focused on sales in the title insurance industry. For our purposes, strategy is a plan to achieve a goal. Tactics are the actions used to implement that plan. For example, pricing is a strategy. Offering discounts for buyers with a prior insurance policy is a tactic. In this first chapter, we provide a list of business strategies available to a title insurance agency and explore the distinction between marketing and sales.

In 1954, Peter Drucker[1] wrote "There is only one valid definition of business purpose: to create a customer. .... Therefore, any business enterprise has two—and only two—basic functions: marketing and innovation. Marketing and innovation produce results; all the rest are costs. Marketing is the distinguishing, unique function of the business."

In 1973, Drucker[2] argued "...selling and marketing are antithetical rather than synonymous or even complementary. There

---

[1] Peter Drucker, *The Practice of Management* (New York: Harper & Brothers, 1954).

[2] Peter Drucker, *Management: Tasks, Responsibilities, Practices'* (New York: Harper & Row, 1973).

will always, one can assume, be need for some selling. But the aim of marketing is to make selling superfluous." In Drucker's view, the job of sales was to overcome objections whereas, "The aim of marketing is to know and understand the customer so well that the product or service fits him and sells itself."

In the book *Market Driven Strategies*,[3] Day makes a distinction among customer oriented, market oriented, and market-driven. Day argues that companies that are customer oriented put the customers' needs and values at the center of their strategy. In essence, it means being customer focused. Being market oriented means understanding the total market, customers, competitor, and market conditions.

The Market-driven organization creates value for the customer by continually assessing customer satisfaction and customer needs and staying ahead of the market by refining its products and services to meet customer needs. Essentially a market-driven company is both customer oriented and market oriented.

Market-driven strategies can be distinguished from actions that focus exclusively on revenue or the profit of a company. For example, cost cutting is a profit driven tactic that benefits the company. Drucker would argue that cost cutting is not a market-

---

[3] George Day, *Market Driven Strategies: Processes for Creating Value* (New York, N.Y., The Free Press, 1990).

driven strategy because it has no effect on the customer or marketplace.

When one examines the tactics used to promote and sell title insurance, it is essential to understand that land title insurance is regulated at both the State and Federal level. At one time, title insurance was nearly the sole practice of lawyers and lenders and the ethics and business practices common to the industry were those of law firms and banks. Marketing and sales, to the extent they existed, were conducted by the principles of the firm and based on relationships. As the industry opened up to new players, sales and marketing expanded and new business practices pushed the limit of the law until illegal or unethical practices like kickbacks were common in some areas of the country.

In 1974, the Real Estate Settlement Procedures Act (RESPA) was enacted by the United States Congress to ensure that the business of transferring real property was conducted in a legal and ethical manner. For some, RESPA created a level playing field. For others, RESPA was one more unwanted restriction forced on the title business.

On July 21, 2011, the administration and enforcement of the Real Estate Settlement Procedures Act (RESPA) turned over to the Consumer Financial Protection Bureau (CFPB). The Real Estate Settlement Procedures Act (RESPA) was created to ensure that consumers are provided with accurate and timely information about the cost of the mortgage settlement and are protected from unnecessarily high settlement charges caused by certain abusive practices. As the industry moves into the digital age, business strategies used by a title insurance agent or underwriter still have to be qualified by the "Does it pass the RESPA test?"

In our experience, the legal strategies and tactics used to promote title insurance fall into one of the following categories:

1. Price
2. Location
3. Customer Service
4. Customer Focused
5. People (expertise)
6. Profit
7. Product (quality)
8. Sales
9. Marketing
10. Branding

Recently, Blue Ocean[4] Strategy and Social Networking each have been proposed as new and distinct strategies. Likewise, some authors argue that technology is a distinct strategy, whereas other

---

[4] R. Mauborgne and W. Kim, *Blue Ocean Strategy: How to Create Uncontested Market Space and Make Competition Irrelevant* (Harvard Business Review, 2005).

authors consider technology to be a tactic that can be used as part of any number of traditional strategies.

Deciding whether something is a strategy or tactic can quickly become rather academic, however social networking is a good example to consider. Social networking in business is a tactic (or method) designed to promote a company or product through a network of customers and friends. It takes advantage of the internet and applications like Facebook. Conceptually, social networking is a form of word of mouth marketing (a very old tactic) using technology to deliver the word to significantly more people. Naturally, as business people experiment with social media they will develop a set of guiding principles and methods that might seem to set social networking apart (as a strategy). However, the same was true of telemarketing and direct mail. In our opinion, social networking is an old tactic with a new method. It is not a new strategy. It is just a new way of marketing (e.g., a tactic).

In *The History of Marketing Thought*,[5] Bartels considers the development of sales and marketing concepts. Many of the initial concepts came from economics. According to Bartels, 1910-1920 was a period of development, in which ideas from economics, psychology, sociology, and scientific management were used to explain sales.

_____

[5]Robert Bartels, *The History of Marketing Thought* (Richard D. Irwin, Inc., Homewood, Illinois, 1976).

In the 1920s, the first textbooks and college classes on sales and marketing were established. This was a period of conceptualization. During the depression and war years, 1930-1950s, marketing concepts were tested and refined. After World War II in the 1950s, business experienced a period of reappraisal follow by a reconceptualization of sales and marketing principles. Authors like Cox, Alderson, and Shapiro[6] redefine marketing principles with more emphasis on sociological, psychological, and behavioral patterns of consumers.

In the 1960s academics, business writers, and leaders in advertising began to focus on the customer. During this period, the prime marketing strategy for a company became differentiation. The assumption was a company had to market product features or benefits that would differentiate the company from its competitors. The role of marketing was to develop a unique way in which a business or product meets customers' needs.

For example, BMW claims it is the Ultimate Driving Experience. It does not claim to be fastest, cheapest, or the best looking. It only claims that all of its vehicles offer the ultimate

---

[6] Reavis Cox, Wroe Alderson, and Stanley J. Shapiro, *Theory in marketing*, (Richard D. Irwin, Inc, Homewood, Illinois, 1964).

driving experience. This is the reason to buy a BMW and the test by which a consumer is to judge their cars.

Differentiation typically takes many forms. Companies try to be different in physical or virtual appearance, in the types of people they hire, their order entry systems, the ways in which they deliver their products and services, and in the value-added services they provide. It is easy for a company to say they are different but much harder to deliver on that promise.

Since the 1960s a number of new marketing theories have emerged, but differentiation continues to be the dominate idea. In our experience, very few title insurance companies can make the claim that they do something unique or innovative. The title insurance policy from any of the major underwriters is essentially the same.

In the past, the features that differentiated a company were its people and its system of records. In New York and Texas we have met Title Officers with near photographic memories of a county's land records. In the past, companies employing such individuals could dominate the market. Even today, some companies still emphasize having a title plant and title officers. The problem is when underwriters sell searched products or searchable court records are made available online, the advantage of having a Title Officer with thirty or forty years of knowledge is lost.

Many title companies combine a number of features (strategies) including knowledgeable people, quality products, and reliable service, along with some type of marketing and sales coverage. In a restaurant or hotel, trying to be everything for everyone (a shotgun approach), often results in customers judging the business to be "Good" or "Average." The same can be true of title companies.

Marketing and advertising are methods designed to make customers aware of a company or product. In essence, the purpose of marketing is getting the customer ready to buy; wanting to buy. Sales is a process designed to overcome objections and close a deal. Traditionally, sales is an interpersonal process in which a customer goes through a sales person to sign a contract or makes a commitment to buy a product. The sales person and the marketer typically do not create or produce the product or deliver services, rather their role is to get the customer ready to buy the product. Any number of business writers[7] have argued that Marketing and Sales have to be in balance. Each needs the other.

What is important about this definition is sales always means people interacting in the process of buying a product. Marketing is everything else. In this distinction, advertising, public

---

[7] http://fusionmarketingpartners.com/resources/white-papers/bridging-the-gap-between-sales-and-marketing/

relations, direct mail, and social networking are all marketing methods to promote a company and its products.

The title insurance industry is rather unique in that it is an old industry with several major Fortune 200 companies, yet its brands are relatively unknown outside the industry even though nearly every homeowner has title insurance. One of the reasons is the underwriters do not advertise; it is an industry that conducts marketing instead of sales, and hires sales people who never negotiate or close. In a traditional model for sales, the sales person is responsible for negotiating price and signing contracts. In title insurance, a representative of the buyer or seller orders preliminary insurance information that will be used when a piece of real property changes hands. If the property is sold and transferred, a fee will be paid for issuing an insurance policy related to the property. What is unusual about this process is a service is requested and delivered without payment, and a product is often ordered without going through a sales person or signing a contract. From an insurance perspective, what is most unusual is the insurance does not protect the buyer from future problems; rather it protects the buyer from mistakes made in the past.

In professional service companies, like lawyers and doctors, marketing brings customers through the door and the practitioner becomes the actual sales person. For example, you select a dentist using the Yellow Pages or Google, and then the dentist and hygienists sell you on a program of dental care. In such business, word of mouth marketing and social networking become critical. The same is true in the title industry. In a professional business there may be no sales person employed by the company. Rather, the company uses marketing and local advertising.

Imagine that you own a restaurant. A person comes in, sits at a table and says to the waiter "I am ordering dinner for a friend," and he wants the dinner served at six in the evening. Then he informs the waiter "My friend will pay for the food when she shows up." At this point, the person walks out. If this was your restaurant would you make the dinner as requested before the customer arrives and risk the situation that no one will show and you will have an unpaid for dinner? Of course, this is what is done in a takeout restaurant where uncollected food is resold, but not in a quality restaurant.

If you owned this restaurant, my guess is you would not start the dinner until a paying customer showed up and placed an order. Yet if you own a title insurance agency, this is exactly what you do all the time. A Realtor calls and says I have a house under contract, please start the title work and send me a preliminary commitment in preparation for the closing, and by the way, if the deal falls through, no one is going to pay you for your work. Crazy? Of course it is, but competition within the title industry has created exactly this situation. Title companies market a product, produced on a promise, for which they hope one day they will be paid. Not exactly the ideal situation for a sales person, which means sales in the title industry is not traditional.

We defined selling as an interpersonal act; it requires at least two people (seller and buyer) interacting. Buying on the other hand does not require a second person (sales person). Today, nearly everything can be purchased without an interpersonal interaction. Not to split hairs, but consider the following examples and decide whether selling is involved.

1. A new Realtor places her first order through your website after seeing the site on the internet.

2. An established customer faxes in a new order when a contract is signed.

3. You sponsor a golf outing and get two orders from the winner of the tournament.

4. You take a customer to lunch and a week later, she calls in an order to the order desk.

In the first example, the company is selling its products with its marketing channel. There is no sales activity. In the second example, a sales person might claim the revenue associated with this faxed order, but habit and the customers' experience have more to do with this sale. In the third example, sponsoring a golf event and even playing golf with a customer are marketing tactics.

If a sales person actually asked for an order at the event and got a commitment, we would call his/her actions selling. In the last example, taking a customer to lunch is clearly sales behavior, but failing to ask for an order at lunch suggests that the layer order is a form of quid pro quo or favor. Favors cannot sustain a business.

When looked at from this perspective, most of the activities of the sales staff in a title company are marketing activities. Unless the sales person is actually asking for an order or taking an order, his/her efforts are designed to make the customer aware of the Company and build a relationship. In essence, they are primarily using marketing tactics for attracting customers.

## GUIDING PRINCIPLES FOR CHAPTER 1

1. Strategy is a plan to achieve a goal.

2. Tactics are actions used to implement a plan.

3. It is easy for a company to say they are different, but much harder to deliver on that promise.

4. The purpose of marketing is getting the customer ready to buy, sales closes the deal.

5. Today, nearly everything can be purchased without a personal interaction.

## DEVELOPMENT IDEAS\QUESTIONS FOR CHAPTER 1

1. Work with your management team to develop a list of company features or characteristics that differentiate your company from competitors. Determine how you can better focus and highlight these features in your marketing and sales activities.

2. How often does your sales staff ask for an order when meeting with a customer? How can you increase that sales behavior?

# BUSINESS STRATEGIES

## CHAPTER 2

In the first chapter, we provided a list of business strategies available to a title insurance agency. In this chapter, we are going to provide a more detailed overview of several of the strategies we introduced in Chapter 1. For each, we will define the strategy, give examples, and discuss our experience with the strategy.

The list of strategies includes:

1. Price
2. Location
3. Customer Service
4. Customer Focused
5. People
6. Profit
7. Product
8. Sales
9. Marketing
10. Branding

PRICE

For any sales person, the easiest and simplest way to make a sale is to offer a product at a price lower than any other company. Wall Mart is famous for this strategy. The problem is there is always the person down the street who is willing to offer a lower price even if it means he and you go out of business. In our view, good companies do not compete on price. Therefore, title companies should never compete on price at least on a residential transaction. Instead of using price, they need to make other considerations for their best customers.

We debated making price the first strategy on the list. In sales, offering a lower price or a discounted price is the last strategy a business should employ. Lowing your price is a move that suggests desperation. It says you have nothing else on which to compete. Yet, offering a good price is the first thing a salesperson wants to do. It is tangible and makes the customer happy or indebted. For most sales people, offering a lower price does not significantly affect their commission so there is no disincentive.

One of the things we learned when teaching phone skills for a catalogue sales company was unless the salesperson had a prepared script that explained the benefits of a product that was higher priced, he/she would immediately offer a lower price. In other words he wasn't prepared to overcome the most basic objection. Rather, he used price.

Competing on price suggests that a business's product is like a commodity, meaning the product is the same regardless of the manufacturer. For example, for most consumers, sugar is sugar regardless of the brand. The same goes for salt. The brand does not matter, only price. Can the same be said of a residential title insurance policy? The last thing that title insurance wants to be is a commodity. As such, agents and underwriters alike should never compete on price for residential title insurance.

## LOCATION

The old joke is "What are the three most important factors in real estate?" The answer is Location, Location, and Location. Today, having an office with good parking that is convenient for customers is essential. In the future, when closings are completed on-line and in the home, location will not matter. Now it can.

If you are a gardener, you are familiar with the idea there are spots in a garden where plants will not grow. Nothing will grow. Likewise, there are locations where no business is successful. You probably know a corner where five restaurants have gone broke. Title companies that are tucked away in a hard to find location with limited parking probably do not survive. Except in New York City, most title companies want to avoid being higher than the third floor of an office complex.

Traditionally, title companies were designed for practicing attorneys. They were located near to the courthouse so records could easily be searched and recorded. In the 1960s, title companies were located near the courthouse or the largest law firm. In the 1990s, companies in the Midwest and West moved nearer the biggest Realtor. Often, like shoe stores, title companies are all on the same street. In some instances, the title company is even inside the Realtor's office.

Today, a good location is determined by how far the target customer has to drive and how easy is it to park and get in and out of the building. We are familiar with a title company on the west coast that was located in the heart of the downtown. A perfect location across from the courthouse. Then the city built a new parking garage and changed the parking meters in front of the company from three hours to ten minutes. This was done to promote the use of the new parking garage just down the street. Now if a customer calls before she comes to the office, she is told to stop and pick up a roll of quarters for the parking garage. This means the customer does not pay for parking, but he/she still walks, two blocks often in the rain.

PEOPLE

Having the best people is a solid strategy for any technical business or service business. One of the complaints regarding technology companies is they have highly trained technical people who understand nothing about customers and customer service. The title industry is both a technical business and a service business. In many markets, having the best closer or best commercial examiner can make a company number one.

Employees with the knowledge and experience to produce, sell, and service a product are essential. With title insurance, having a good search / examiner and a good closer might be all that is needed to compete. Having the top closer can move an average company into the top three.

Issuing title polices is a technical profession. Currently, most transactions require knowledge and experience with the local laws and practices. A top sales person is expected to bring in 3 to 5 times his/her salary. Estimates are that the cost of a bad hire is three times the salary paid. According to Amy Rees Anderson in Forbes online[8], "great employees are not replaceable."

When you think about the business that a top closer or a great title examiner retains, you realize what Anderson means. Top performers make other employees perform. Rogers likes to say, mediocre leaders, create mediocre companies, whereas great managers and employees can create a great company.

Collins, in his book Good to Great[9], argues that in order to build a great company, one that is "built to last," you start with the people and let the people create the processes and structure. Unfortunately today, the title industry invests very little in people. Generally, often due to necessity, salaries are low and there is little

---

[8] (http://www.forbes.com/sites/amyanderson/2013/02/13/great-employees-are-not-replaceable/
[9] Jim Collins. *Good to Great* (New York: Harper Collins, 2001).

formal education and training available. Most employees learn on the job rather than by formal and effective training.

## PRODUCT TYPE

Earlier we said that the title industry is at risk of becoming a commodity, in essence, a title policy is the same regardless of the underwriter or agency. Within the industry, there are long and short policies, refinance policies, and commercial policies. In each case, what is covered is different and what can be underwritten varies. For the residential buyer and seller, there is something called an owner's policy and a lender's policy. In each case, the policy covers the risk (money invested) to the buyer and the lender. Behind the veil, the process to create each type of policy is the same and while they are different legal documents, they cover the same property and the same set of facts.

What varies is the quality and carefulness of the work. In New York and on the east coast where attorneys purchase title reports and then perform the closing based on the commitment, the accuracy of the title commitment and settlement figures makes the difference between a happy buyer and seller and a lost customer. In these markets, the company with an accurate product may be able to make a difference. In many markets, errors in the commitment occur because of improper initial data and the pressure to get a commitment out in days if not hours. In these markets, errors are common and are corrected as they are found, often by checkers before final commitment typing.

For most buyers, a title policy is something the bank requires and it is not clear what would happen if the banks stopped requiring a lender and owner's policy. Certainly, buyers and sellers would use a settlement service, the question is would they actually purchase title insurance in the process?

In the commercial world, the underwriting can be different and the title search and examination process are essential. Most commercial properties require a loan and no loan would be approved without title insurance. In essence, commercial transactions require a title policy.

## CUSTOMER SERVICE

Great service is never an accident. Companies that deliver consistently great service usually have great people and great systems to support them. In most title companies, great service, if it occurs at all, happens because of a single hero. Meaning the customer receives great service because one person goes out of her/his way to make it so. Such individuals always put the customer first even if that means taking advantage of other employees. In profiling title employees, we have found that these customer service people have a behavioral profile of a perfectionist. In our experience, many of the top closers are perfectionists. This means that they set a very high standard for their work and for customers. It also means they may chew up other employees making sure everything is perfect for the customer. In these hero companies, the service might be great, but the culture is very negative. Ideally, a company hires people with great service skills, who really care, and then the company provides the employees with the training and tools to do what is right and best for both the customer and fellow workers. Great service should not be a sacrifice. Rather, it is a well-oiled professional process.

## CUSTOMER FOCUS

There is a difference between companies that are customer focused and ones that deliver great customer service. Customer Focus means understanding a customer's wants and needs and producing and delivering products the customer wants or needs. Customer Focused companies conduct customer research and evaluate customer satisfaction. In a customer-focused company, the customer is always right and the products and services are developed around the customer. Customer Service, according to Danny Meyer[10], is in part, the mechanical delivery of the correct product to a customer at the correct time, place, and price.

---

[10] Danny Meyer, *Setting the Table: The Transforming Power of Hospitality in Business* (New York: Harper Collins Publishers, 2006).

When title insurance was created, it was developed for attorneys. The commitment was written for lawyers in a language that lawyers understood. Even today, the modern commitment and title policy are written in a form and language adapted more for lawyers than Realtors, lenders, or buyers and sellers.

In many companies, considerable expense has been applied to making the closing experience a positive one for those attending closing. This is an example of good customer service, but not customer focused, because it ignores the obvious question: Why do we have to close at your office?

Taking a step back, the products, procedures, and practices of the average title company may have little to do with good service or what the new customer wants or needs. In our experience, procedures used in the typical title company are 5-50 years old and were designed around the people who do the work. They are procedures that make it easier for the employee and little to do with the customer or great service.

A customer focused approach results in products and services designed around a target customer's needs and desires. For a detailed discussion of these two strategies, read our chapters on Customer Service and Customer Focus.

## GUIDING PRINCIPLES FOR CHAPTER 2

1. The last thing title insurance wants to be is a commodity. You should not compete on price.

2. As more and more closings are completed online, location will not matter.

3. Having the best people is a strategy for success.

4. Great service is never an accident. Companies that provide great service have great people and systems.

5. Customer focus means understanding and delivering what customers want and need.

## DEVELOPMENT IDEAS\QUESTIONS FOR CHAPTER 2

1. Review our list of strategies. Which of these basic strategies are you currently using? What additional strategies do you use that are not on our list?

2. For each strategy that you use, how are the tactics used to implement the strategy different from your competitors? Which strategies have resulted in the best results? Which have not? For those strategies that are not producing the needed results, what should be eliminated, improved or changed in some way?

3. After you have completed reading *Finding the Right Strategy*, consider the additional sales and marketing strategies you want to implement. Develop an action plan to develop and improve the sales strategies and tactics you use.

# BRANDING

## CHAPTER 3

A company is a brand when customers associate the name or logo of that company with their need for a specific product or service. In this chapter, we examine what it means to be a brand, the history of brands in the title industry, and we consider the components of brand development and brand management for a title agency or underwriter, including the importance of advertising directly to the consumer.

### WHAT IS A BRAND

A product is a brand when customers associate the name of that product with a specific need. Originally, when Kleenex was developed it was a facial tissue for removing cold cream. Over time, people used it to blow their noses and found Kleenex to be easier and cheaper than handkerchiefs. Now, when you have a running nose and need a facial tissue, you might ask for a Kleenex, but that does not mean you buy Kleenex or are loyal to the brand. Kleenex has become the generic name for a facial tissue. This may be the ultimate stage of branding, but it does not necessarily result in increased sales.

Consider for a moment your local dry cleaners. Roger has been going to the same dry cleaners for over twenty years. By any measure, he is a loyal customer and they are a successful local business. The question is, are they a brand; do they have brand identity or brand differentiation?

You might argue they have to be a brand because they have stayed in business for more than twenty years. The only problem is Roger had to look up their name (Deluxe) and he would go to a different dry cleaner if they were as close and offered the same one-day service. Roger's loyalty is not to the company and he has no identification with the brand.

Most successful companies create loyalty among a unique set of customers. However, our point is customer loyalty is not the same as having a brand. We know many Realtors who will only close at one title company, yet their loyalty has nothing to do with branding, they are loyal to a person; the closer or sales person in that office. Becoming a local or an industry brand requires more than loyal customers.

Some companies are respected brands within an industry, but are barely known to the public. For example, Johnson Controls is a global diversified technology and industrial company serving customers in more than 150 countries; it has 170,000 employees. If you work in batteries or hotels you know about Johnson Controls, yet most people know nothing about it because they have no direct buying experience. Here in Chicago, Rick Bayless and the Frontera Grill are very well known by foodies, but less known outside of Illinois or among the general public. However, now that Bayless has a line of products in grocery stores across the country, his own cooking program on public television, and has won the title Top Chef on a different national television program, he, and his companies, have become a distinct brand.

The title insurance industry appears to be one of those old industries that has one foot in the digital age and the other still in the 1900s. Advertising before the 1920s consisted of billboards, word of mouth, and newspaper and print advertising. In many ways, the title insurance industry has never moved beyond this form of marketing and advertising. The majority of local title companies relies on signage, print ads in trade journals, and name placement by sponsoring real estate events. We know only of a few exceptions like John Martin in El Paso, Texas, who uses television and radio to advertise his title company.

In the 1920s, Radio changed the nature of marketing. Products and brands became associated with entertainment. In the 1950s with the introduction of television, strategies used in radio were transferred to television. The Lux Radio Hour became the Lux Video Hour and finely the Lux Playhouse.

In 1955, the Leo Burnett agency[11] began a new ad campaign for Marlboro cigarettes. Before the ads, Marlboro was considered a "minor brand marketed for their mildness and aimed at women

---

[11] http://en.wikipedia.org/wiki/Advertising

27

smokers." Burnett created the Marlboro Man, with images of cowboys on horses, smoking "a cigarette designed for men that women like." These images combined with Elmer Bernstein's theme from the movie *The Magnificent Seven* made Marlboro the best-selling cigarette brand and the Marlboro Man became an icon for the brand. This form of marketing associates copy text and images with a product in order to create a Brand. The images and copy used in the Marlboro ads changed the brand's image and audience.

In contrast to the branding approach used by Burnett, Rosser Reeves assumed that images could be confusing. He felt what was important was to articulate the product's critical feature. Reeves wrote about his views in his 1961 book, *Reality in Advertising*[12]. Reeves argued that the purpose of advertising is to sell. He believed that you sold a product by showing its unique properties repeatedly. He is famous for his ads for the headache medicine Anacin. The ad with its pounding hammer and anvil was considered grating and annoying but it tripled sales. Reeves believed that once you found a winning way to advertise a product you kept with that approach. He also believed the ad had to be honest. He insisted the product being sold actually be superior to

---

[12] Rosser Reeves, *Reality in Advertising* ( Knopf, 1961).

its competitors. Reeves hated what came to be called creative advertising in the 1960s or content advertising.

In contrast, in the 1960s, David Ogilvy created a number of successful ads, including the Man in the Hathaway Shirt, Schweppes, Rolls Royce, and the island of Puerto Rico. The idea of content marketing was the ad was information-rich, but used a 'soft sell' approach.

Consumer psychology became important in the 1960s. Marketers began to interview and survey customers in an attempt to understand the psychology of the buyer. One famous example is when Psychologist Ernest Dichter and copywriter Sandy Sulcer learned that motorists desired both power and play while driving. Their campaign to "put a tiger in your tank," for Exxon Mobil gave the consumer an image that fit with their desire or need.

As advertising advanced into the Digital age, "guerrilla marketing" began. This type of advertising is unpredictable and innovative, which causes consumers to buy the product or idea. Examples of guerrilla marketing are staged encounters in public places, giveaways of products such as cars that are covered with brand messages, and interactive advertising where the viewer can respond to become part of the advertising message via text messages or social networks like Facebook or Twitter.

It remains to be seen whether the title industry will advertise at the national level. With the rise of more self-directed consumer behavior driven by the internet and social networking platforms, it is likely only a matter of time. With this in mind, it is helpful to understand the distinctions among brands at the national level like Pepsi, with industry brands like Johnson controls and local brands like Frontera Grill in Chicago.

In the title industry, the national underwriters like Fidelity, Chicago Title, or First American are certainly major public companies and they are recognized industry brands. Certainly, they are industry leaders and people in real estate know them. What is surprising is for an industry with over one hundred and fifty years of serving home buyers and sellers, the national underwriters are largely unknown to the public.

Why is this? First, the national underwriters do no national advertising. They do not market or sell their products to the public. Second, inside the industry, their products have little to distinguish them. A title policy is the same whether written by First American or Stewart Title. Finally, they use a shared network of local agents to sell their products. Meaning most agents have more than one underwriter. Therefore, the agent is not going to promote one underwriter over another, he/she is going to establish his/her agency as a dominate local or regional brand. Because multiple underwriters use the same agent to sell and deliver a similar product, there is little basis for the Realtor or homebuyer to know or remember Chicago Title and every reason to remember the local agent.

For example, Rattikin Title is a very well known title company in Ft Worth Texas. Here is what Rattikin says about its history:

> Rattikin Title was officially formed in 1944 by Jack Rattikin, Sr. and his wife, Annie Lee Rattikin, whose business philosophy was based on dedication and service to their customers. That same philosophy continues to guide the family today, as the company is presently owned by the Rattikin family.

> Today, Jack Rattikin, Jr. is the Chairman of the Board, Jack Rattikin, III is President of the title company, and his brother Jeff manages the Rattikin law firm. What sets Rattikin Title apart is that it is the only family-owned title company in Tarrant County. Rattikin Title is a well-known local brand with three generations (70 years) in the business.

Most companies start as a local business and become known and loved by a small group of devoted customers. Some of these local brands expand into other locations and other companies. This step is precarious and most small business fails in this step. Even fewer companies become a regional company or national. Often, when a company goes regional or national, it loses its brand identity or its identity becomes diluted. This can happen for any number of reasons, but a change in ownership or leadership is the probably the most common reason. In the title industry, the major national underwriters grew out of local businesses, and as they grew and changed owners and leaders, they have lost much of what made them different.

Effective branding is a type of differentiation that gives a company a competitive advantage. Mention the words The Ritz Carlton and a superior level of hotel service and experience immediately comes to mind. If you are successful at branding, your brand says who you are, this is what your company stands for, this is what makes you different, and this is what you can count on. If you are successful in developing an effective brand, the brand's image is what customers automatically associate with your company.

DEVELOPING A BRAND

A brand can be the company or a product. Brands are created by a combination of consumer word of mouth, advertising, marketing, and sales. A local brand can be developed over time by word of mouth alone (think the Soup Nazi in the comedy series Seinfeld), but developing a national brand, in our opinion, requires mass exposure, consumer usage, marketing and advertising. Becoming a brand is something that happens over time.

Toyota began in 1933. Toyota was a well-established automaker in Japan when it entered the American market in 1957. By the 1980s, Toyota was an established brand with a family of cars. It had in the Corolla, a top selling car that would one day become number one. What Toyota did not have in 1989 was a luxury car to compete with a Mercedes. Creating a new brand is an expensive idea. Brands need a name, a catch phrase, a logo, a look, features that people want, a distribution system, and a culture that wants to sell and serve.

In the 1980s, all of the major automakers in Japan were making luxury cars in Japan. In 1986, Honda introduced the Acura line using an existing car from Japan. Mazda and Datsun did the same. Toyota sent its researchers to conduct consumer research in the U.S. They concluded that a separate brand and sales channel (dealerships) were needed to present a flagship luxury sedan.

The actual car was developed by a special design team and would be manufactured in its own plants. According to Wikipedia, the name Lexus developed out of over 200 names. At first, Alexis was going to be used, but was changed to Lexus. The word has no meaning. Next a slogan was developed, "*The Relentless Pursuit of Perfection.*" Then, the Lexus logo was developed. Finally, the car was launched at the North America Auto show in Detroit. That debut was followed by a multimillion dollar advertising campaign. Ultimately, Car and Driver claimed the Lexus 400 was better than both BMW and Mercedes and that year sales of the two European automakers dropped significantly. In the end, Toyota did what it intended. It created a lasting luxury brand that competes directly with Mercedes and BMW. What is clear from this history is creating a new brand is not cheap or easy. Nor is it a sure thing.

Creating a new brand identity for an existing company has its own set of challenges. For example, Bell Labs existed before their name was changed to Lucent. Bell Labs spent considerable money to change its name and look, and separate its self from AT&T.

Here is a black and white version of the logo for Lucent Technologies, now formally Alcatel-Lucent. The actual logo is red. Lucent was created in 1996 when AT&T, Western Electric, and Bell Labs were de-merged. AT&T still exists and has its own identity with consumers.

For a time, Lucent's stock did very well, even if the average American still called them Bell Labs. Perhaps what is most interesting is their logo. Here is what Wikipedia has to say:

> The Lucent Logo, the Innovation Ring, was designed by Landor Associates, a San Francisco-based branding consultancy. One source inside Lucent says that the logo is actually a Zen Buddhist symbol for 'eternal truth,' the Enso, turned 90 degrees and modified. Another source says it represents the mythic Ouroboros, a snake holding its

tail in its mouth. The Lucent's logo also has been said to represent constant re-creating and re-thinking.

After the logo was compared in the media to the ring a coffee mug leaves on paper, a *Dilbert* comic strip showed Dogbert as an overpaid consultant designing a new company logo; he takes a piece of paper that his coffee cup was sitting on and calls it the "Brown Ring of Quality". A telecommunication commentator referred to the logo as "a big red zero" and predicted financial losses.

Having a new name and a new logo does not change the culture of a company. Likewise, having a name and a logo does not create a brand. Chicago Title has been in business for over one hundred and sixty years and it has a gold castle as a logo.

The Chicago Title Logo was inspired by that age-old saying, "A man's home is his castle." The castle signifies the homes that we insure. However, the ring around the castle is of even greater significance - it is emblematic of a moat. Just as a moat protects a castle's walls, the circle around the castle represents the protection you receive from a Chicago Title Policy. The turret motif of the logo is modeled after the old Chicago Water Tower, one of the few edifices to survive the Great Chicago Fire.

In the 20 plus years we have worked with Chicago Title, we have only met a handful of managers who talked about the logo and its meaning. Certainly, employees and customers wear clothes with the logo and have business cards and letters with the logo. Unquestionably, if you showed the logo to most Realtors or real estate attorneys, many would know the name of the company. However, if you asked them what the logo means or how the logo represents Chicago Title, or how Chicago Title is different from First American, we believe you would have mostly blank stares. Why is it that some brands or logos have become so identified with the product they become the industry name for the product and others never catch on?

Kleenex was the first facial tissue. For many Americans, Kleenex has come to mean all tissues. According to Wikipedia:

> **Kleenex** is a brand name for a variety of paper-based products such as facial tissue, bathroom tissue, paper towels, Tampons, and diapers. In the United States, Kleenex is a generic term for all facial tissues. *Kleenex* is a registered trademark of Kimberly-Clark Worldwide, Inc. The Kimberly-Clark Corporation created the first Western facial tissue in 1924 and originally marketed them as a way to remove cold cream or makeup remover... It was a disposable substitute for face towels. In 1925, the first Kleenex tissue ad was used in magazines showing "the new secret of keeping a pretty skin as used by famous movie stars..." By the 1930s, Kleenex was being marketed with the slogan "Don't Carry a Cold in Your Pocket" and its use as a disposable handkerchief replacement became predominant.

Many products have strong Brand identity without becoming a generic. For example, McDonald's, Burger King, and Big Boy are all successful brands. Each is distinct. The question is if you want a burger, do any of these come to mind. For many American's, and around the world, McDonald's golden arches means burger, yet in New York City, the Shake Shack means burger and in San Francisco and Las Vegas, the Burger Bar is king.

The McDonald's Corporation is the largest chain of hamburger fast-food restaurants in the world. According to Wikipedia, it serves 68 million customers in 119 countries daily. For many consumers McDonald's is generic for burgers or fast food. Certainly, the company logo, the Golden Arches, has come to represent the Brand.

Roger was in college when the first McDonald's and the first Burger Kings were introduced in Kalamazoo. Today it is hard to imagine a city without a McDonald's, but back then, they were new and competed head to head on taste, location, and price. McDonald's was close to campus and offered fried burgers for a quarter. Burger King was out by the new Mall and offered a double sized char grilled burger called the Whopper. The Whopper cost more, but offered more meat. In the 1970s, Burger King claimed to win on taste. McDonald's competed on price, and had great fries. Both offered a fish sandwich that was, in hindsight better than their burger.

If you consider the two major families of title insurance underwriters today, Fidelity and First American, neither company advertises and neither has a strong brand identity with homeowners or the public.

If you asked the average home owner they probably could name the agent or office that closed their home, but it is unlikely he/she would be able to name the underwriter or explain what they do, or describe the difference among the companies. Why? First, because title insurance is only marketed to real estate professionals: Realtors, Lenders, Builders, and Attorneys. The second reason is the local business is promoting its brand over the underwriter.

A company's name or a product can develop into a brand by accident or it can come about by a plan. Whichever path, the process of developing a brand starts with the basics. At their core, all brands start with a purpose and customer experience. These elements start to form brand identity:

1. We have a product we want to sell.

2. We bring customers in contact with the product.

3. If the product meets the customer's goals, the customer will buy again.

4. As the customer continues to use our product, he/she will associate fulfilling his/her need for the product with our company name and company symbols, e.g., logo, thus creating brand identity.

## MULTIPLE BRANDS

When a company has more than one brand, they are said to have a Portfolio or a Family of Brands. For example, Frito-Lay,

Inc. is a division of PepsiCo. Frito-Lay manufactures, markets, and sells corn chips (Fritos and Cheetos), potato chips (Lay) and other snack foods. Fritos, Lays, and Pepsi are each examples of Brands and members of a family of Brands. Each Brand has its own products, its own customers, and it is different in some meaningful way from its competitors.

A Portfolio can either consist of a Family or House of Brands (e.g., GM has Buick, Chevrolet and Cadillac) or the company develops a Branded Family or House, that is where all the brands use the Company name, (e.g., Virgin Records, Virgin Airlines, etc.). Today, only Fidelity is an example of a Family of Brands with Fidelity National Title Group: Fidelity National Title, Chicago Title, Ticor Title, Alamo Title, Commonwealth, and Lawyers Title.

Brands can be primary, meaning that they are a main name or product. If a brand is not primary, then it is a sub-brand or a line. For example, General Electric (GE) is a primary brand, whereas GE Monogram and GE Profile are sub-brands of GE. Using this distinction, Metropolitan Title was a sub-brand of First American.

A primary brand can be extended, for example, Diet Coke is an extension of Coke. As an alternative, brands can endorse, that is the brand lends its identity to a new product line. The iPod is an example of an endorsed brand, i.e., the Apple brand endorsed the iPod. In the case of the iPod, it may now be the Primary Brand. The Talon Group at First American was an example of an endorsed brand. In the simplest formula, a Company has one brand with one product, competing in one category.

COMPANY → BRAND → PRODUCT → CATEGORY

Until recently, Stewart Title and Old Republic were the only major underwriters with a single brand. First American is in the process of moving from multiple brands to one brand. As of this writing, Fidelity is the only major underwriter using multiple brands selling the same products to the same customers in the same markets.

Managing multiple brands requires clarity about the brand fundamentals, positioning, and strategies. More than anything, such complexity requires strong brand leadership, brand management, and an understanding of the culture of the company and the image that the company holds with consumers.

Generally, when a company offers two brands, providing the same product it wants to ensure that the two brands have different customer targets, markets, or that the features and/or benefits of its products speak to different customer needs. Ideally, each brand has its own group of customers and different competitors.

One of the dangers for a company with multiple competing brands is that the brands will cannibalize each other rather than taking market share from their external competitors. This is called having a Redundant Brand. An example of this problem may have been New Coke and Traditional Coke. New Coke was designed to go after Pepsi customers, but may have only attracted existing Coke customers.

Ticor Title may be an example of a strong brand that became redundant; however, for some, a better description was cannibalized. When Ticor was first purchased by Chicago, it had its own identity, its own business practices, customers and markets. However, over time, the acquisition resulted in the brand differences fading. Eventually, customers reported to us that there were no differences in the personnel, services or products compared to the Chicago Title brand.

Sometimes, a brand dies because it is a poor or underperforming brand. When a company has poor performing products or brands, the poor performing entity may bring down the name value of the primary brand. The recent fall of General Motors and the elimination of the Oldsmobile is a good example of this problem. In essence, consumers could not see the difference between an Oldsmobile and a Buick and Oldsmobile's lagging sales were bringing down the GM name. In the case of First American, the poor performance of United General and Talon made each brand a drain on the parent.

A further danger for a company with a family of brands is when one of the brands does not live up to or follow the standards or the foundation of the parent. For example, a few unprincipled managers in one division of Arthur Anderson destroyed the entire company. Cases involving illegal practices in California, Colorado, and New York all speak to this issue among the major title underwriters.

## BRAND MANAGEMENT

The success of any brand depends on a number of factors: leadership, management, culture, products, quality, price, customer perceptions, marketing, and sales. Long-term, the most important factor in determining a company's success is continuity of leadership.

Additional factors that are critical for a company's long-term success are its culture; the people, their relationship with customers, and the way that work is performed. More than anything else, the leadership at the senior level and culture of a company (the behavior of employees, managers, and agents at the local level) shape the customers experience with a company and form the Company's image in the market place.

According to published sources, First American's strategy for the future is to become America's real estate data source, whereas Fidelity National Financial appears headed towards becoming the backbone of the financial services industry. However, the last six years (2008-2014) have brought about considerable change. In 1990 there were over nine major underwriters all offering the same things to real estate customers. Today there are only four major companies: Fidelity, First American, Stewart, and Old Republic.

In examining the four major underwriter groups, it appears that First American has essentially dropped its different brand names and created business divisions whereas Fidelity continues to have multiple brands. Stewart and Old Republic operate as title underwriters and collectively control about the same share as First American. As brands, Stewart has been recognized for its technology and Old Republic has become a brand for agents. In the next ten years, it is hard to say what changes will occur in the industry let alone what brands will remain.

The development of a brand, at its simplest, is creating a reliable association of a customer's experience with a company and its products. For example, Roger has owned an Apple IIe, Macintosh, iPod, iPhone, and iPad. He trusts the company and likes their products. On the other hand, he has purchased six Windows based computers and he has used the Windows Office

Suite for over twenty-five years. You might say Roger identifies with the Apple brand and its innovative products, but he is not entirely loyal because he owns other computers and likes the Windows Office Suite. This situation may be a little like the one faced by Fidelity and First American. They are the brand leaders and people have experiences with both and like both.

To help you strengthen or develop your brand, consider the following questions.

### Brand Questions

1. Why was the company started?
2. How was the brand created?
3. What is the purpose for the brand?
4. What are the values that underlie the brand?
5. What are the brand's products?
6. Who are the brand's target customers?
7. What are the customer goals that the brand fulfills (frame of reference)?
8. What are the brand's target markets?
9. How are the brand's products distributed?
10. Does the Brand have directs and agents?
11. If the brand has agents, who are the brands target agents?
12. How are the brand's products marketed?
13. What is the brand's message?
14. What is the brand's intended image?
15. What do customers actually perceive the brand's image to be?
16. What is the brand's strategy to grow revenue / customers?
17. Who are the brand's actual and intended competitors?

18. What is the brand's actual and intended position?

19. What is the brand's price point?

20. What is the brand's expected and actual market share?

21. What is the brand's expected and actual profit level?

22. How is the brand managed? What is the management structure?

23. How competent are the brand's managers?

24. How is the brand led? What are the leaders' strengths and weaknesses?

25. What is the current culture of the company? Has the culture changed?

## GUIDING PRINCIPLES FOR CHAPTER 3

1. A company is a brand when the customer associates the name or logo of that company with a particular need.

2. Becoming a local, or industry brand requires more than loyal customers.

3. Often, when a company goes regional or national, it loses its brand identity or its identity becomes diluted.

4. Effective branding is a type of differentiation that gives a company a competitive advantage.

5. Having a name and a logo does not create a brand.

6. The national underwriters do not have a strong brand identify with homeowners or consumers.

7. With the rise of the internet and more self-directed consumer behavior, it is only a matter of time before the title industry will turn to more direct advertising.

8. At their core, all brands start with a purpose and customer experience.

9. What matters most is whether customers have experiences with the brand that are consistent with stated values.

10. Managing multiple brands requires clarity about the brand fundamentals, positioning, and strategies.

11. The most important factor in determining a company's branding success is continuity of leadership.

## DEVELOPMENT IDEAS\QUESTIONS FOR CHAPTER 3

1. Is developing for your company a local, regional or national brand, or brands, important to you? Have you already created a brand name, image and consistent customer experience for one or more of your brands? Would developing or further developing one or more brands provide your company with important marketing and sales strategies?

2. If the answers to any of our above questions are yes, review the brand questions on pages 44-45. Meet with your management team to discuss each question that pertains to your operations. For each question, determine what needs to be developed, improved or changed in some fashion regarding your branding strategies.

3. Develop an action plan for your branding strategies based on your review and discussion.

# CUSTOMER SERVICE
## CHAPTER 4

In this chapter, we consider how Customer Service has been used as a strategy to increase sales. In the past, legal knowledge and product quality, meaning the accuracy of the title commitment and policy, gave a company a competitive edge.

For the first one hundred years, the title industry was dominated by lawyers and lenders. Title companies focused on what lawyers wanted and needed to complete a real property transfer. For example, a standardized title policy form first appeared in the 1920s because lenders wanted one form.

In the 1980s, Chicago Title prided itself on the quality of its underwriting. They believed the lawyer or agent wanting to do business with them had to take what they offered because they had few alternatives. For the purpose of our discussion, they were far from being Customer Focused or Customer Service oriented as a company could be. In fact, they probably turned customers away because the customer did not meet their criteria of a good customer or agent.

Today product quality is more likely a threshold feature, meaning if you do not have an accurate product you will lose customers, but accuracy alone is not enough to gain or keep most residential transactions. Keeping residential Realtor customers is all about service.

Service is one of the few factors on which title companies continue to compete. If you think about calling on a potential customer, a target, a title company sales person has himself/herself, the product (meaning quality and knowledge), and service to sell. Among those three strategies, we like to say the sales person brings the customer through the door, the product can lose a customer, but service is what keeps and brings a customer back. Therefore, having good service is an essential feature (tactic) in any marketing or branding strategy.

In the 1990s, when First American and other underwriters like Fidelity entered into markets dominated by Chicago Title and Ticor, their sales force offered different (easier) underwriting, they offered better (lower) fees, and they spent more time and money on coverage and marketing to new customers. In contrast, Chicago spent considerable money on loyal, high volume agents, but it ignored small agents and it charged higher fees for all agents because it believed its underwriting was superior.

For a while, being number one was enough to keep customers. Eventually Chicago and Ticor lost customers to First American's and Fidelity's aggressive marketing. At first, Chicago countered by focusing on turnaround time, meaning they tried to be faster (first) with a commitment. Ultimately, they implemented a series of tactics designed to enhance Customer Service.

In the 1990s, CBA offered our first seminar on customer service based primarily on the books *At America's Service: How Your Company Can Join the Customer Service Revolution* by Karl Albrecht and *Raving Fans* by Kenneth H. Blanchard and Sheldon Bowles. In our training, we emphasized getting the basics right and recognizing moments of truth, those moments where a service failure will cost you a customer. As good as our training was we knew that it lacked some key element, something to connect all the different ideas on exceptional service at the time. It was not until Chris Hanson and his wife were dining at one of their favorite restaurants in New York City, Union Square Café, that the missing element became clear. Here is the story.

Chris and his wife Cheriann had eaten at Union Square Café (USC) on several previous occasions. They knew the restaurant was known for great food, had won several awards, and was very popular, but so were many other restaurants in New York at the time. On this particular night, something happened that set Union Square Café apart and solidified their loyalty.

Union Square Café is wedged into what looks from the outside to be a small storefront at 21 East 16th street. Only steps away from Union Square, the café opened its door in 1985. Inside, the restaurant is warm and inviting with a large dining room, steps

51

below the street level. After being greeted and seated by the upbeat front room staff, their waiter promptly delivered menus and said he would be back in a few minutes. Sitting in the smaller front section of the restaurant, Chris was quietly studying the dinner selections when Cheriann said,

"I am so disappointed, the polenta crusted sea bass is not on the menu tonight. It is one of my favorites and I was looking forward to it."

Acknowledging her disappointment, the two discussed the menu selections for that evening. Minutes later, their waiter returned, and asked if they wanted to order drinks and did they have any questions about the menu? Since there were a number of great items on the menu, neither one of them mentioned the missing item from the menu that had so disappointed Cheriann. However, not long after the drinks arrived the waiter reappeared carrying a warm dish that he set down in the middle of the table between them. To their surprise, he announced that he had overheard Cheriann's disappointment about her favorite dish, and had asked the chef to prepare a special appetizer for the couple containing many of the same ingredients from the missing menu item. As you might imagine, they both looked at each other with big eyes and huge smiles and said "WOW!"

Months later, we read an article in a Gourmet magazine by Bruce Feiler that talked about the owner of Union Square Café,

Danny Meyer. It turns out that the staff in each of Meyer's restaurants are trained in dozens of ways that will create an exceptional experience for customers. For example, they even practice how to put out a fire at a table when birthday wrapping paper is exposed to too many birthday candles. For us at CBA, it was this idea of creating a system of little surprises and service WOWs that was missing from our basic customer service training. Using the concepts discussed in the article on the Union Square Café, we developed the idea of WOW customer service training for title agencies. The core idea we started with was training basic customer service in title and escrow and then adding a dozen or more service WOWs, critical moments, designed to WOW a customer.

In 2006, Danny Meyer explained his philosophy of leadership and management in his book, *Setting the Table: The Transforming Power of Hospitality in Business*.[13] In the book, he makes a distinction between service and hospitality. According to Meyer,

> Service is the technical delivery of the product. Hospitality is how the delivery of that product makes the recipient feel. Service is a monologue, we decide how we want to do things and set our own standards of service. Hospitality on

---

[13] Danny Meyer, *Setting the Table: The Transforming Power of Hospitality in Business* (New York: Harper Collins Publishers, 2006).

the other hand, is a dialogue. To be on a guest's side (customer's side) requires listening to that person with every sense; following up with a thoughtful, gracious, appropriate response. It takes both great service and great hospitality to rise to the top.

Meyer goes on to say, "Hospitality cannot flow from a monologue. I instruct my staff members to figure out whatever it takes to make the guests feel and understand that we are in their corner." Just like Chris' experience with the waiter bringing his wife a special dish, from the customer's perspective, the net effect of several WOW experiences is a lasting impression that results in more sales and glowing recommendations to other potential customers.

In Danny Meyer's restaurants, people are hired because they show a number of critical personal characteristics that exemplify Meyer's vision of hospitality. Once hired, the wait staffs are trained in every aspect of exceptional service, but more importantly, they are taught to listen and create a dialogue with customers. After their training, they are able to deliver dozens of exemplary service actions, designed to fit the particular situations with which they are faced on a day-to-day basis. Even after working in the restaurant, employees continue to receive training and feedback on their performance. In monthly staff meetings and daily pre-dinner discussions, they are encouraged to introduce new ideas, always with the goal of making the customer's experience a WOW.

Since 2002, CBA has offered WOW customer service training for title agencies that focuses on teaching title staff and managers how to develop and implement customer service actions that will WOW customers on a repeated basis. In our workshops, we draw a comparison between title companies and restaurants. In both, you schedule a table over the phone, greet the customer in a lobby, and take the customer to a table. In both cases, a customer places an order that requires a largely unseen professional staff to prepare a product. Then a separate staff delivers your product to the customer. In both examples, the service staff interacts with the customer, and at the end, there is a bill for the product and services. Naturally, the comparisons break down at some point, for example, tipping is frowned upon in the title industry, but in our experience title companies could learn much from the innovations seen in some of the great restaurants and hotels in the last 20 years.

In an industry in which the product, title insurance is almost a commodity, it is critical that all employees understand the importance of building customer relations through sales and service. For too long, title underwriters and title companies have believed that what mattered to the majority of customers was having an accurate title policy and the financial security on which it is written. Of course, performing an accurate search and a detailed examination along with conducting a professional settlement are important, but from the consumer's perspective, the work required is unknown and the fees charged at the closing seem unjustified.

For most buyers, the title policy is a set of papers that come after the closings and have no relation to the fees charged at the closing. In some states, the policy is issued at the table, whereas in other states the policy might arrive months later. From the homeowner's perspective, the policy is just another document added to a file of 'important papers.' In general, we might say that the title policy has little or nothing to do with the buyers' opinion about the services performed by a title company.

Historically, title companies considered their customers to be intermediary (a customer representative) who ordered the title work, whether, attorney, lender, or Realtor. Many years ago (1992) when Roger closed a home in northern Illinois, he was informed that he would need an attorney, lender, and a Realtor, even though in southern Illinois he purchased a home without an attorney. Being a new consultant, with Chicago Title as his major client, Roger made it clear to his Realtor that he wanted to have the title policy written on Chicago Title and the closing held at the Geneva office where Roger had spent four days learning about the ins and outs of a title office. Surprisingly, when Roger's Realtor called with the address for the closing, he learned it was in Naperville, some 20 miles from his new home. To make a long story short, when Roger arrived at the address he learned that it was a First American office and his Realtor and Attorney had completely ignored his requests, because in northern Illinois, the seller selects the title company. Furthermore, to add insult to injury, Roger discovered that because he was late (having gone to the wrong office) his closing would have to be completed in the hallway because the sellers' attorney had another closing. All of this was explained to Roger by the sellers' attorney while holding his own personalized coffee cup taken from a wall in the FATCO office. Needless to say, Roger has told this story many times when he wants to talk about customer service in the title industry.

To start, title companies have to realize that there are anywhere from one to a dozen potential customers in every closing and giving one person or group preferential treatment during the closing would be like serving hot food to the restaurant critic and cold food to his guests. During the closing, the buyer and seller are the most important people in the room because they are paying for the settlement. Beyond this simple fact, it should be clear that if the buyers or sellers are unhappy with the title company or the closing experience, they will hold their attorney, lender, and Realtor responsible. During the closing, like during the dinner at a restaurant, the goal is to complete the transaction with no hassles and to have everyone leaving happy. To have this happen on any single closing should be possible. All it takes is an exceptional closer and the dedication and hard work of the title and closing departments working together, along with a little luck. To have this happen on nearly every transaction is not easy, and yet great hotels and great restaurants make it happen every day. So why is it that most title companies, like most businesses in America, only give mediocre service most of the time? The answer is they lack the leadership, management, training, and systems necessary for delivering dependably good, let alone great service, on every transaction.

## CUSTOMER SERVICE BASICS

Let's look closer at the differences between good and great customer service and start by emphasizing Danny Meyer's distinction between hospitality and service. In a restaurant, customer service involves those technical things that you do with an order to deliver the right food at the right time to the right table. Good customer service is about preparing good / safe food and delivering what the customer ordered.

In a title company, good customer service means producing an accurate and timely title product and services to the parties participating in a land transaction. Good customer service means getting the names and addresses correct, performing a timely and accurate search, it means properly examining the chains of title, and having all the documents correct and complete at the time of the closing. Beyond these basics, good customer service requires answering the telephone and e-mails correctly, it means providing a clean, comfortable, and private place for the closing, it means greeting customers on arrival, and it means having clean restrooms and refreshments available for customers. It means having a website that is informative and helpful, it means having employees who are friendly, polite, and who care more about the customer than themselves. It means a hundred other little things that must or may happen when a customer is interacting with your company. Good customer service means meeting the customers' expectations and occasionally going beyond. Great customer service is something more, and adding hospitality to great service is that much harder.

In our training, we like to say that great customer service begins with getting the basics right and having a smart plan for correcting problems when things go wrong. Customer service basics are as simple as smiling and being friendly. The basics can be taught, but it is easier and wiser to hire people with good basic skills, rather than think you can train an old dog new tricks. What follows is a list of basic service behaviors:

Basic Service Behaviors:

1.  Active listening
2.  Asking questions
3.  Being accurate
4.  Being courteous
5.  Being efficient
6.  Being friendly
7.  Being helpful
8.  Being knowledgeable
9.  Being polite
10. Being proactive
11. Being prompt and timely
12. Following through on what was promised
13. Getting the details right
14. Knowing what the customer needs or values
15. Recovering from a mistake
16. Showing positive energy
17. Smiling
18. Solving problems
19. Staying calm
20. Using a positive "can do" voice
21. Using eye contact
22. Using positive body language

In a title company, these basic service behaviors should occur behind the scenes and during critical points of customer contact. For example, in the lobby or reception area customers expect certain service basics. They expect the receptionist to smile, to offer a friendly greeting, to answer questions, to be helpful and to make the customer comfortable. In addition, offering a snack or beverage and having a clean restroom greatly enhance a customer's experience. These are all basics. Every area in a title company and every feature or function in a transaction has some basic service requirement. Great companies start by getting the basics right. But, getting the basics right only keeps you in the in the game.

If a company wants to deliver great customer service, it has to dedicate itself to raising the standards of every employee and replacing those employees who fail to meet or live up to the standard. To get started, we recommend taking our basics list and add, edit, or delete behaviors from our list. The point is to identify your functional areas (like reception) and within each functional area identify critical points of customer contact. After you have a list of expected behaviors and a list of areas where the behaviors are expected, you may want to evaluate the level of basic customer service that is occurring in each functional area or simply assume that all employees need some training/review of service behavior in each area. Consider the areas or functions listed below. Take each area and list the service behavior expected in that area or function.

61

Areas and Functions in a Title Company

1. Sales contacts

2. Web site

3. Order entry over the phone, by fax, e-mail, on-line

4. Title production, search, examination

5. Creating a commitment

6. Policy production and delivery

7. Escrow production

8. When discussing clearance issues

9. Reception

10. During a closing

11. When dealing with children

12. In the bathrooms

13. In common and food areas

14. Communications

15. On the telephone

16. In e-mails

17. On faxes

18. When interacting with any employees

19. When interacting with management

20. When providing information or file status

21. Transmitting policies

If you look at your own company, you will probably be able to identify those areas where your service is strong and those areas that are weak or lacking some basic element. For example, answering the phones. In most title companies, if they have more than one office, it is very likely the phone is answered differently in each office. Consider for a moment, these three examples:

1. Good morning, how may I help you?
2. Good morning, Clear Title, how may I direct your call?
3. Clear Title, this is Betty.

What do you think about each of these responses? What would you keep and what would you change? In our phone training, we consider each of these examples less than perfect. In our opinion, the response we look for includes the salutation, the company name, the person's name, and an offer to help. For example:

1. Good morning Clear Title, this is Roger, how may I help you?

When we present this response, we usually get a lot of debate about each element and we always get a group who argue that it does not matter, or there is no need to answer the same way in each office. More recently we have heard that customers do not have the time to listen to a long greeting. So, who is right? Of course the answer is the customer. The only problem is that most title companies have never asked a customer and the average customer experiences such poor service, in general, that being friendly and polite are taken for superior service.

Every title company has a few people who really care about customers and service. Because of a few, most customers experience good service, and occasional great service. Imagine would happen if every employee cared about customers and was dedicated to service.

In great companies, Nordstrom is an example, people are hired for their customer service attitude and skills and then they are trained to deliver on the technical aspects of the business. In most title companies, it is just the opposite, people are hired because they can examine or close and then the owner and manager tries to manage the service problems and baggage the employee has carried over from their last employer. Of course, one solution is hiring people with great service skills to begin with.

CORRECTING MISTAKES

In America, receiving the wrong product or bad service can often be turned into a good service experience by simply saying "we are sorry, we are at fault, and here is what we are going to do to correct the problem." Owning up to your mistakes will take a company a long way. Learning from your mistakes and making fewer mistakes can put a company in orbit. In a sense, recovering from a mistake is just another basic, but a very important basic in some industries. We recommend identifying a list of common problems or mistakes your company will likely experience over a period of time. For each problem you identify, develop a standard procedure that will be followed to not only correct the error, but leave the customer with a positive impression. Danny Meyers[14] calls this writing a great last chapter. He writes:

> The worst mistake is not to figure out some way to end up in a better place after having made a mistake. We call that "Writing a great last chapter...To be effective, the last chapter must be written imaginatively, graciously, generously, and sincerely." (pp. 222).

---

[14] Danny Meyer, *Setting the Table: The Transforming Power of Hospitality in Business* (New York: Harper Collins Publishers, 2006), pp. 222.

## GUIDING PRINCIPLES FOR CHAPTER 4

1. Customer service is one of the few factors on which title companies continue to compete.

2. Having good service is an essential tactic in any branding, marketing or sales strategy.

3. Moments of truth are those critical points of customer contact where a service failure will cost you a customer.

4. Service is the technical delivery of the product, hospitality is how the delivery of the product makes the customer feel.

5. CBA offers customer service training that teaches title staff and managers how to develop and implement customer service actions that will wow customers on a repeated basis.

6. There are from one to a dozen potential customers in every closing.

7. Great customer service starts with getting the basics right.

8. If a company wants to deliver great customer service, it has to dedicate itself to raising the service standards of every employee.

9. Recovering gracefully from a mistake with a customer is another form of basic customer service.

# DEVELOPMENT IDEAS\QUESTIONS FOR CHAPTER 4

1. Work with your management team or a customer service team to review the CBA basic customer services list. Considering your operations, what additional basic service behaviors should be added to the list?

2. Review the CBA Areas and Functions list. Add to the list any additional areas from your operations where basic customer service is important. To help you review where service basics are important, identify the critical points of contact (i.e., moments of truth) throughout the order transaction process in your company.

3. Take your basic service list you developed in #1 (above) and ask the following question for each functional area you identified in #2 (above): Which of our basic service behaviors need to occur in each of our functional areas? List each functional area and the corresponding service behaviors that need to occur in each area.

4. With your teams and using your basic service lists, evaluate the current level of service in each functional area.

5. Based on your assessment of your basic service levels, develop an action plan for improvement. What training is needed? Which employees are below standard in terms of their customer service performance? How will training be provided? How will you continue to evaluate whether consistent basic customer service is being provided in each functional area?

# WOWING CUSTOMERS

## CHAPTER 5

Once a company has mastered the basics, you might ask whether the company needs to go beyond the basics? In fact, if a title company got the basics right on 80% of its transactions it would own the market. So the question is do you need to go beyond the basics? Our answer is not until you really have the basics right.

In our experience, getting the basics right is more than 80% of the battle and it is the most difficult challenge for a company. Getting the basics right requires leadership, employee acceptance and commitment, skills training, management participation, new service procedures and systems, on-the-job practice, and rewards and incentives, and effective hiring. When employees are getting it right, they are happy and customers are elated. According to Danny Meyers,[15]

> If you are trying to provide engaging hospitality and outstanding technical service, there must also be a certain amount of fun involved...I watch my staff members. Are they enjoying one another's company? And are they focused on their work? If the answer to both questions is yes, I feel confident that we're at the top of our game." (p 51).

---

[15] Danny Meyer, *Setting the Table: The Transforming Power of Hospitality in Business* (New York: Harper Collins Publishers, 2006) pp. 51.

Going beyond the basics might be the least expensive thing a title company can do, because going beyond the basics is a little like adding the topping on a great cake. After all, if the product is accurate and on time, the closing starts on time, the documents are correct, and employees are positive, upbeat, friendly, and polite, what more is required? The focus of this chapter is going beyond the basics to provide exceptional service as a strategy.

## WOWING CUSTOMERS

Ask yourself, "What wows me?" Make a list of examples and for each example, see if you can derive a principle about consumer behavior. As psychologists, we know that people have different likes and dislikes. For an adult, our experiences growing up combined with our genetic makeup results in a person with a few unique characteristics and many shared characteristics. Because of our common or shared characteristics, we are able to profile people and group their behavioral tendencies. For example, people who are risk takers and people who are list makers. Basic to buying behavior, we know there are a limited set of factors related to wowing people. For example:

1. People are Wowed when Price is low and Quality high

Many shoppers are price sensitive and are wowed by low prices, good deals, and bargains. These shoppers might enter a Walmart, look at the low price of a jumbo tube of toothpaste, and say, "Wow." Other shoppers seek value, meaning the balance between the quality of a product or service and price.

On the other hand, some shoppers never look at the price, and as such are not wowed by a low price; in fact, the lowest priced items may be something they avoid. These shoppers may never shop in a Walmart and even if they do, they might not be wowed by all the savings.

In a title company where pricing is regulated, it might be hard to wow a customer on price, but there is always the unexpected.

2. People are Wowed when unexpected positive events are free.

People are wowed when they unexpectedly receive something of value or something they like. Roger remembers the first time he stayed in a room and the matches in the ashtrays had his last name printed on them. WOW. Roger was the chair of a committee picking a hotel for a state conference and apparently, the hotel manager wanted to impress Roger and influence his decision. In looking at this example, several features should be considered.

First and foremost, Roger was wowed because seeing his name printed on the matches was so unexpected. He had never seen or heard of this now common marketing trick. The other factor to consider is the use of Roger's name. Clearly, some people are pleased when their name is used in certain situations and upset when used in others. For example, Roger likes it when people call him Dr. Lubeck but he hates being called Rog or Lu. The manager tapped into something basic in Roger if not everyone. At the same time, there were some risks. First, Roger did not smoke so he might never have noticed the matches. Second, as flattered as he was, he did not select the hotel. The point being that great service and wowing the customer does not always create a loyal customer.

Recently Roger stayed at a new hotel in Las Vegas and the room key had his name printed on the card. Again, for Roger this was a WOW. Thirty years later, he is still saying "WOW" when his name appears unexpectedly on items.

Like using a person's name, we know that some people love it when there is free candy in a meeting or expensive soap in a hotel room. In these examples, the fact that the item is unexpected may be entwined with the fact that it is free.

3.  People are Wowed when service seems personalized.

Shoppers frequently talk about the level of assistance they receive as being a potential wow factor. For example, Roger is a very direct shopper. He knows what he wants and generally he does not need help nor does he want assistance. He very much dislikes it when a clerk in a woman's store thinks he cannot pick out clothes for his wife. On the other hand, he appreciates it when the salesman in the suit department brings him several suits to consider. Contrast this with an executive we knew who had his personal buyer meet him at Sacks Fifth Ave after they had closed so he could buy his clothes privately. This executive would buy a season's worth of clothes because of the recommendations of his buyer. The meeting at Sacks was only to be sure of the fittings.

Superficially, Roger and this executive are very different, except you might say both expect their sales person to understand and cater to their unique needs. You might conclude that some buyers are wowed when their sales person reads them as individuals and adjusts their sales behavior accordingly. This principle is called individualization or customization.

4. People are Wowed when service seems individualized.

In addition to individualized service, most consumers are wowed when the salesperson or service person goes out of his/her way to help or assist the buyer. In may be important that the event

73

is unexpected. For example, years ago at the Union Square Café, they decided they would have spare umbrellas at the door for guests who have forgotten their umbrella and are caught in the rain. When they gave out their first umbrella the guest was surprised and wowed. Now, having takeaway umbrellas is common at many restaurants, both fine dining and friendly neighborhood establishments.

At one time people were wowed by air travel and they dressed up to fly. Today, the average traveler arrives in jeans, a tee shirt, and slip off shoes. As consumers grow use to an innovation, we have to add something new, unexpected, surprising, and pleasing. Once a wow is expected, it probably ceases to wow and yet its removal may still be negative.

WOW EXAMPLES

Below is a list of wow examples and the underlying wow principles they represent about consumer behavior. Along with each principle, we have added a title company example. In determining what could be wows in your title company, we recommend returning to the functional areas list you considered for service basics. For each functional area and critical points of customer contact, identify possible wow actions to take. Below are examples of seven actions that will Wow.

We recommend starting by developing three to five wow actions for each of your functional areas. Once you have identified the wow actions, you will need to train employees on how and when to perform each action. The training will have to ensure an action is applied consistently and occurs as part of an ongoing service dialogue with your customers. Once a program of Wow is implemented, you will want to monitor for results so that planned actions can be updated, revised, or have new actions added.

Action 1: A sales person listens and then says something that shows he\she has listened. Wow Principles: Listening well; providing confirmation; understanding customer preferences. Title Co. example: A sales person provides a written summary to the customer about specific actions title and escrow production will take to improve service for the specific customer.

Action 2: I see that someone has gone out of their way or above what is expected. Wow principle: Going the extra mile. Title Co. example: An escrow processor takes the extra step to call a new Realtor agent to explain and go over specific documents that are needed from the agent's seller.

<u>Action 3</u>: An interaction is personable and does not seem "staged." Wow principle: A personable dialogue takes place that is uniquely hospitable. Title Co. example: The closing office receptionist welcomes the couple who have come for their closing. The receptionist refers to them by name, leads them to a comfortable area, offers them a drink, and comments on a unique aspect of the home they are selling.

<u>Action 4</u>: I receive something that is extra to what would normally be expected. Wow principle: Added value. Title Co. example: After receiving an order from a new Builder-Developer customer, the manager calls the customer to invite him to come to an office staff meeting and talk to the staff about his business. The new customer meets the office personnel who will be working on his orders in the future, discusses business needs, and gets a free lunch!

<u>Action 5</u>: From the minute I walk in the door, I feel relaxed, at home, that the business represents an extension of me. Wow principle: Shared identity. The closer arranges items and procedures in the closing room that the customer (e.g., Realtor agent) has indicated as preferences: favorite drinks; a welcome to the community packet that has the agent's material in it; and, an opportunity for the agent

before the closing starts to make personal introductions and comments.

Action 6: I enthusiastically tell a friend about my history with an exceptionally good company website. Wow principle: Emotional attachment. Title Co. example: a customer raves to a fellow business associate about how a title company's website allows users to track the progress of an order and a help-line feature that provides immediate access to a knowledgeable title professional. The customer refers to the title company as "his title company."

Action 7: I feel cared for, looked after, that the company is on my side. Wow principle: The business actively has the best interests of the customer in mind. Title Company example: The title company provides the customer with periodic legislative updates and news and instructions for new rules and regulations. The company shares it's newsletter with the customer. The company invites the customer to a business social to meet other business leaders and customers in the area.

## ADDING HOSPITALITY TO GREAT SERVICE

Hospitality often happens in the moment and it takes the skill of the employee to essentially read the situation at hand and be spontaneous. At the table in a restaurant, a waiter must be able to read the table and respond accordingly. Likewise, at a closing table, the closer needs to look for opportunities to be hospitable, especially during introductions, and at the very end of the closing. As we have mentioned, Danny Meyers likens the concept to creating a dialogue with the customer. Servers in his restaurants must read the situation in front of them and respond in creative customer focused ways.

This is not to say, however, the concept of hospitality cannot be taught to employees directly. It should be. One excellent way we know of is to constantly provide and discuss examples of hospitality with your employees. The Ritz Carlton hotel chain is famous for, in their weekly meetings, encouraging employees to provide examples of great customer service stories, most all involving some type of outstanding hospitality. These stories get circulated among the company and act to provide excellent models employees learn from and in their own ways learn to adapt to the situations they encounter. We encourage you to make sharing great customer service stories a part of your on-going company culture.

## PUTTING IT ALL TOGETHER

Improving your overall customer service and occasionally Wowing customers is a strategy to increase sales. The strategy starts with getting the basics right, and that requires training.

Train basic customer service. We recommend that a company trains service behaviors and routinely manages to them. Develop a list of basic service behaviors that employees should exhibit in each of the functional areas of your company.

Provide hospitality. Once employees understand basic service, they have to be trained in the concept of providing hospitality. Hospitality means listening to customers and engaging customers. It means creating a welcoming environment and responding to the needs of the customer (Customer Focus).

Deliver WOW experiences to the customer. The final step in our process is learning how to WOW customers. Start by developing a list of WOW actions you will use in the different areas of your company. Train your employees to provide these Wows routinely. If you follow these three basic steps, you will be using a proven strategy for increased sales.

## GUIDING PRINCIPLES FOR CHAPTER 5

1. Getting the service basics right is the most difficult challenge for a company.

2. Going beyond the basics may be the least expensive action a company can take to improve its competitive advantage.

3. People are wowed with the price is low and the value is high.

4. People are wowed when unexpected positive events are free.

5. People are wowed when service seems personalized or individualized.

6. People are wowed when employees go out of their way to assist the customer.

7. Hospitality happens when you create a spontaneous, unique dialogue with the customer.

8. The concept of delivering hospitality to customers should be taught to employees directly.

9. All great customer service stories involve some example of hospitality.

DEVELOPMENT IDEAS\QUESTIONS FOR CHAPTER 5

1.  After you have customer service basics provided at consistently high levels, turn to training the delivery of wow service experiences and hospitality.

2.  Meet with your management or customer service teams and start with discussing examples in your operations of providing hospitality. Review your functional areas list and identify examples of hospitality in each of the functional areas of your company. Write out your examples and have them ready to use in training. One idea is to develop role-plays for hospitality training.

3.  Provide hospitality training directly to your employees in two steps: (1) Train the general concept of hospitality: employees need to be able to read the situation in front of them with the customer. They need to be able to react to the situation at hand in spontaneous ways that takes into account what can be personalized or individualized with the customer, in an ongoing dialogue; (2) Use the hospitality examples you have developed to aid in the training. Enlist employees to role-play different customer hospitality scenarios for the different functional areas of your company.

4.  Next, turn to the development of wow service behaviors. Work with your teams to identify specific wow actions that can occur in each functional area. Start with a small number of wow actions (e.g., 5) that can be consistently delivered by your employees. Develop standard procedures to follow for each wow action. Your teams can develop new wow actions and procedures throughout the year (e.g., 2-3 new wows per quarter).

5. Train employees to deliver consistently the wow actions you have developed. Train by using the step-by-step procedures you have developed.

6. Discuss with your team how you will monitor, manage, and evaluate the delivery of hospitality and wow actions.

7. Consider using measures of customer satisfaction to evaluate your overall levels of customer service, hospitality, and wow.

8. Use the idea of discussing great customer service stories as a way to improve your overall customer service culture. Distribute and discuss your great customer service stories in various ways throughout your company.

# CUSTOMER FOCUS
## CHAPTER 6

As business psychologists, we believe that a successful salesperson combines her knowledge of the product with her understanding of customers. To be effective in sales, knowing the product is not enough and understanding the customer is not sufficient. When used together the skilled sales person is prepared to sell a product she understands to a customer she understands.

In our experience, there are at least two kinds of sales people. The sales person who convinces a potential buyer to buy a product regardless of whether he/she needs the product and the sales person who takes the time to determine what the potential customer wants and needs and sells him/her a product that meets those needs.

The first approach is called High Pressure Selling. We call the second approach Consultative Selling. It is also called being Customer Focused. Customer focused companies determine what a customer wants or needs and then develop and sell the customer the product or service he/she needs or wants. This chapter examines understanding what customers' value and the tactic of aligning sales behavior with customer behavior.

Taken to its logical extreme, Customer Focused companies are driven by what the customer wants, need, or tells them he/she needs. They offer products and services designed completely around the customers' needs and desires.

If a title customer (Realtor) said, "Can you send a limo to pick me up for a closing at your office?" a Customer Focused company would send a limo. Of course, this is a RESPA violation and more importantly, it is a foolish and unprofitable idea. In the title industry, a company can be Customer Focused only up to a point. The company has to follow the law, they have to consider what is best for the industry, and they have to make a profit.

In our opinion, being Customer Focused means 1) knowing what customers <u>you</u> want (qualifying); 2) understanding what the customers you want need; and 3) designing and delivering products and services that legally and financially meet those needs. To be customer focused, you first have to determine what type of customer you want (Qualify). Consider for a moment that you are a new sales person and you have your choice of calling on one of several potential customers:

1. Existing customer, 12 closings a year with you, claims to be very satisfied.

2. Partial-customer, 12 closings a year, 6 with you, 6 with a competitor, very satisfied with both companies.

3. Non-customer, 6 closings a year with a competitor, claims to be satisfied.

4.  Non-customer, new to business, 3 closings in first 6 months, claims no affiliation.

In our experience, customers who receive the most sales attention often are the ones who need the least sales attention. For example, Customer # 1 is a loyal, highly satisfied customer. Marketing and sales are all about getting a customer through the door and getting the person to buy. If a customer is highly loyal and already buying they do not require sales attention, they require consistent great service.

Sales research[16] suggests that increasing retention by a small percentage can result in substantial increases in revenue. This makes Customer # 2 a good target because he isn't completely loyal. On the other hand, research has demonstrated that very satisfied customers are hard to change. Based on this finding, it may be difficult to get more business from Customer # 2. Many people prefer having a choice or fall back. Customer # 2 may be dividing her business as a practical response to the market. The fact she is highly satisfied means it will be hard to change her buying behavior. Customers # 3 and # 4 represent the best opportunity. Neither is highly satisfied and together they represent more business than is lost from Customer #2. So why is it that so many sales men and women avoid going after new customers and spend

---

[16] Frederick F. Reichheld, *The Loyalty Effect* (Harvard Business School Press, 1996).

so much time on established customers? The answer is it is easier to call on someone you know who likes you (Customer # 1). In addition, they probably receive a commission for Customer # 1's business even though the customer has become a "house account".

Effective sales require that we identify the customers we want (criteria) and go after existing and new customers who meet that criteria. In our experience, if you are going to call on new customers, it is important to understand what type of customers you want and make sure the new potential customer meets your criteria (Qualifying). A new customer has to be right for the company and for you, the sales person.

On Roger's first day as a business consultant, he attended a lecture given by one of the top commercial attorneys in Chicago. In his presentation, the attorney argued that selling title insurance to attorneys was easy because there were only two types of attorney, the smart ones, and the dumb ones. After considerable laughter, he asked the audience of title professionals which type they wanted as customers. In the discussion that followed, he made it clear that the smart attorney was more demanding and in the end would cost more than her/she might be worth. This observation is supported by research on loyal customers. Loyal customers can be highly demanding and expect a discount on price when possible.

From this, he argued that the best title customers, whether the attorney or Realtor were those people who did not really understand the business and needed a title professional to do their work for them. Of course, one problem with this argument is often it is the smart attorney or the persistent, careful Realtor who has the business you want.

## MATCHING CUSTOMERS TO SALES

Recent research conducted for e-Harmony appears to have showed that couples who meet online via some form of date-matching process have better relationships and marriages than people who met and dated in the more traditional way, meaning blind dates, met in church or a bar. As Psychologists, we are not really surprised by this finding. For years, we have been profiling people at work and matching compatible behavioral styles in an effort to create better functioning teams. Likewise, for years we have advised that the best way to sell is to match the sales person's behavioral style to the style of the customer.

For example, if the customer wants a lot of detail and time to think before making a selection, don't send in your fast talking high pressure sales person. Instead, pair the customer with a sales person who is steady and careful in his\her demeanor.

We believe that one of the best sales tactics is to match the customer with a sales person. This Customer Focus tactic requires understanding the customer's needs and buying habits and finding a way to change the sales person's approach or behavior to match the needs of the customer. The alternative is to pair each customer with a specific sales person whose style already matches or is compatible with the customer's needs.

Invariably, when we ask sales people about sales tactics, they report relationship selling is one of the most important sales tactics they use. This response has not changed in 20 years. Of course, how the customer relationship gets started, how it is maintained, and what the customer values in the relationship may be quite different for different people and the nature of social relations may be changing. The fact customers have different needs and concerns underline what we believe to be paramount in relationship selling: the key to understanding customers is knowing what they value.

Consider the two following scenarios. George is a customer prospect. He recently visited your website. On your home page, he noticed a YouTube video that highlighted what other real estate professionals in the community had to say about your company. George liked the video and decided to check you out further by clicking on the LinkedIn icon at the bottom of your Home page. Having viewed your LinkedIn profile George contacted you via e-mail to inquire further about your company services. You responded back via e-mail thanking him for the inquiry and indicating you would call him ASAP. George texted you back on his smart-phone to suggest a video teleconference with him and two of his key staff. Several days later, after the video conference, you had a chance to meet face-to-face with George. In the meeting with George, you talked about George's business, his background, and his recent interest in learning to fly a plane. In conversation, you learned that George was thirty-two years of age and had been in the industry for about seven years. At the end of the meeting, George asked if your company had a blog or a twitter Hash tag where he and his staff could follow you.

Now, consider another customer. One day you receive a handwritten personalized note left at your front desk by a customer prospect, Beverly. The note says she would like to talk about a business opportunity. Before responding to Beverly, you inquired about her from a local attorney who you knew had done some business with her. You found out that Beverly had been in the industry for over 20 years, but had worked almost exclusively with a competitor of yours. The attorney friend indicated that Beverly was "old school" as he put it, but a very productive and active Realtor. You quickly decided you would make the effort to reach her by phone and go to her office for a visit the first chance you had.

These two prospective customers have very different profiles, yet in each case, we want to establish a relationship whereby the customer trusts our company and uses our company. The premise of this chapter is before you make a sales pitch you should know what your customers need and value. You have to understand the customers' buying tendencies and sell to his/her needs. To accomplish this we recommend interviewing prospective customers in a process that determines his /her buying style and needs.

The alternative to matching your style or approach to the customer is to present the same style or pitch and let the customer decide if they like you. Much of the history of sales is made up of a sales person delivering the same sales pitch to as many people as possible. The theory was that if one person did not want what you had to sell the next one would and you could make money as long as you made your pitch to a large number of potential buyers. Henry Ford was fond of saying that you could have any color car as long as it was black.

Roger once worked with the owner of a title company who taught sales to Realtors. He believed you should only call on a prospective customer three times. In the first visit, he would get to know the customer. In the second visit, he would make his pitch, and in the third meeting, he would ask for an order. His rule was never more than three contacts. When Roger asked 'why only three sales calls', the owner said, "If a prospect isn't smart enough to do business with me after my pitch, I don't want the customer." This attitude is an example of trying to make the customer fit your mold. In our mind, it is an old fashion way of selling. If it matters, the title company owner who shared his three-visit strategy with Roger is no longer in business.

We believe the best way to gain a new customer is by finding out as much as you can about the customers' business and his/her needs. Customers today are more educated than ever before and have more information available to them to help them choose a company and its products. When a person buys a home, they have the choice of Realtor, attorney, lender, appraiser, and title insurance company. Certainly it is true the title insurance policy is little different from one insurer to the next, but the overall experience with any title company can be very different and the buyer, seller, or her representative, the Realtor, has many choices when it comes to selecting a title company.

## ALIGNING SALES BEHAVIOR WITH CUSTOMER BEHAVIOR

We have made it clear that it is important to understand a customer's behavioral tendencies and match the sales person with the customer's needs. The point is to adjust your sales style or approach to meet the specific behavioral tendencies of the customer. If you know you will be interviewing a specific type of customer, you will be able to tailor your approach to that person's style.

As Psychologists we know that people have patterns of behavior (behavioral tendencies) that can be observed. We also know that certain tendencies go together. For example, people who like to make lists are usually careful. In 1928, William Marston published *Emotions of Normal People.*[17] In this very influential book, Marston argued there were four basic personality (behavior) types or styles. His work was the basis for the DiSC system that exists today. Since that early work, psychologists have debated whether there are four, eight, or sixteen styles, but few would dispute that that number of styles are limited and that in certain situations each unique style will behave in a very predictable way. For example, if a person is careful and organized at home, he/she will be careful and organized at work. Likewise, just as there are careful people, there are people who should not pack a parachute.

In our consulting, we like to say that past behavior is the best predictor of future behavior. In our first book, *Finding the Right Path: A Guide to Leading and Managing A Title Insurance Company*[18], we discussed how managers can adjust their behavior to meet the behavioral tendencies of the people they supervise. The same concept holds true for sales people and their customers, or in fact, for any employee who is planning to meet with a customer.

---

[17] William Marston, Emotions of Normal People. (Taylor & Francis Ltd., 1928).

[18] Roger Lubeck and Chris Hanson, *Finding The Right Path: A Guide To Leading and Managing A Title Insurance Company* (Sugar Grove Illinois: iiWii Press, 2011), pp. 133.

Some business authors have referred to this idea as getting in synch with the customer. If the customer's pace is faster or slower than your pace, adjust your pace. If he wants to get right down to business, get right down to business. If the customer wants to chat, take a few minutes to chat. Consider the following example.

Jim is a salesperson at a local title company. Jim is outgoing and very social, he has excellent people and social skills, but he is not good with details or getting quickly to the point. He likes to talk title over lunch or golf. Jim prefers to start conversations slowly by engaging the customer in some type of a social discussion, often talking about sports. Carol is a prospective Realtor customer (target). You want Jim to interview Carol, to qualify her and make a pitch for her business. Carol is fast-paced, outspoken, and skeptical. She does not like a lot of small talk and prefers you get to the point. She is results oriented and has in the past asked you questions about your turn-time for a title commitment, and how quickly she can obtain updates on orders.

If we were preparing Jim for his interview with Carol, we would tell Jim that he needs to understand that Carol is results oriented. Jim should quickly describe the purpose of his visit and accomplish that purpose as quickly as possible. During the meeting, Jim will need to read Carol's behavior and make sure he is holding her attention. In the end he must make it clear what his company has to offer and ask for an order.

Understanding customers is easier if you have a framework for understanding each person you meet. We recommend using the Everything DiSC Sales Action Planner by Wiley. The Everything DiSC is a commercially available system designed to help sales people evaluate their behavior tendencies as well as customers. When used in the context of sales, the DiSC enables sales people to align their behavior to meet the behavioral tendencies of their customers.

GUIDING PRINCIPLES FOR CHAPTER 6

1. Companies that are customer focused determine what a customer wants or needs.

2. In our opinion, being Customer Focused means 1) knowing what customers you want (qualifying); 2) understanding what those customers need and want; and 3) designing and delivering products and services that legally and financially meet those needs.

3. If a customer is highly loyal and already buying they do not require a great deal of sales attention, they require consistent great service.

4. One of the best ways to sell is for the sales person to adjust their behavioral style to meet the behavioral style of the customer.

5. A key in relationship selling is to know what customers value.

6. The best way to gain a new customer is by finding out as much as you can about the customers' business and his/her needs.

## DEVELOPMENT IDEAS\QUESTIONS FOR CHAPTER 6

1. Go to http://www.onlinediscprofile.com to learn about the Everything DiSC system and consider its use with your management and sales teams.

2. Learn and study your own DiSC profile.

3. Contact CBA to help you learn about the DiSC system and its use with your staff.

4. Once you have become familiar with the DiSC system, use the following DiSC strategy as a quick way to assess the behavioral styles of your customers:

   a. Does this customer tend to be more: **Fast-paced and Outspoken** or **Cautious and Reflective?** (Choose one)

   b. Next, does this customer also tend to be more **Questioning and Skeptical** or **Accepting and Warm?** (Choose one)

   c. Combine the person's tendencies to determine his\her main DiSC style among these four choices: **D: (Direct):** The customer is fast-paced, outspoken, questioning, and skeptical. **I: (Influence):** The customer is fast-paced, outspoken but accepting and warm.
   **C: (Conscientiousness):** The customer is questioning, skeptical, and cautious. **S: (Steadiness):** The customer is accepting and warm, but cautious and reflective.

5. Have your sales people develop DiSC profiles for their customers. Discuss how they can adjust their behavioral styles to better align their sales tactics with the behavioral styles of their customers.

# CUSTOMER INTERVIEWS

## CHAPTER 7

If you want to find out what a customer needs, expects or values, the simplest thing to do is to ask. In terms of asking customers, we suggest a simple structured business/customer interview. Such interviews take thirty minutes to an hour to complete. As simple as it sounds, very few people in the title industry take this direct approach. Rather than learn about the customer, they think they already know, or they assume because a customer is buying from them, they are meeting the customer's needs. This chapter provides a step-by-step approach to interviewing customers.

Taken alone, interviewing customers may not be a marketing tactic. Customer interviews are not meant to be sales calls. Rather, their purpose is to discuss the customer's business, what the customer needs and values, and how you can assist them. Interestingly, often times the customer is so impressed your company is taking the time to sit down and discuss with them what they want and need, the visit results in an order.

To prepare for and implement customer interviewing, we recommend the following steps.

Customer Interviewing Steps

1. Target which customers you will interview.
2. Decide how many customers to interview.
3. Develop a set of interview questions.
4. Determine who will do the interviews and how the interview responses are documented.
5. Practice your interview questions and procedures before the start of interviewing.
6. Contact customers to schedule interviews and develop an interview schedule.
7. Conduct the interview.
8. After each interview is completed, debrief what you have learned.
9. Provide a thank you to each customer in the form of a thank you letter or e-mail.
10. Once all your interviews are completed, combine your findings and analyze the results.
11. Consider providing additional feedback to the customer group interviewed.
12. Integrate your findings with your marketing and sales plans. Include designing an evaluation process to determine if your interviewing results were effective.

## SELECTING CUSTOMERS TO INTERVIEW

In selecting customers to interview, you have to decide whether you are going to interview only your customers, a mix of customers and non-customers, or only non-customers. When we interview customer groups, we are really looking for two distinct things. One we want to discover what is unique about each person and second we want to determine what is common to a group or type of customer (segment). Information unique to a customer will provide you with individual sales tactics. Information common to a group might provide you with a strategic advantage with the segment.

It is likely you serve several different customer groups, for example: attorneys, Realtors, and lenders. When you plan to interview customers, we recommend you develop a set of common questions for all customers and a smaller set of unique questions designed for specific types of customers. For example, questions designed for an attorney will be different from those designed for a lender. In the end, products and the marketing and sales that support a product are designed around what is common. This way we maximize our sales for the least effort and cost. If we interview ten attorneys, they are likely to have much in common, along with various differences. For those attorneys, we can design a product or service to address what is common.

If we interviewed one attorney, a Realtor, a lender, a buyer, and a seller, it is likely they will have little in common except expecting good service and a hassle free closing. In selecting customers to interview, we want to form a group (sample) of people that have something in common. This is called a target or focus group. Once we have decided on the group to interview, we have to determine how many people to interview.

Generally, unless the total number of customers in a market (population) is small, you will have to sample the population by selecting a smaller, but representative group. For example, if there are five hundred Realtors in your market, it is impractical and unnecessary to interview all Realtors. Statistically, a sample size over fifty people begins to approximate the population. The question is can you and do you need to interview fifty Realtors? Fifty in a year may be possible, but is impractical and you do not need to interview that many people.

According to the 80/20 rule, 20% of your customers account for 80% of your income. The same rule applies to all customers in the market. If this is true, you can narrow down the number of customers you need to interview by applying the 80/20 rule. If there are a total of 500 Realtors in your market, odds are that fewer than 100 Realtors account for 80% of the title revenue in your market. One hundred Realtors is still too large a group to interview, but now sampling 20% of 100 becomes a manageable number particularly if a large number of the sample are customers you already serve.

Suppose for example that you have a list of 200 Realtor customers with whom you do business. It would be great if you could interview every customer, but that would be impractical and unnecessary. Using the 80/20 rule, we know that approximately 40 Realtors out of the 200 matter in terms of repeat income. Out of the other 160 Realtors, there are probably another 20 to 40 customers who have potential or are customers with more business to give. Interviewing 80 customers would take months and is impractical at best. What is needed is a sample of customers derived from the group of eighty.

In this case, we said we have 40 Realtors who are our best or "A" Customers and 40 Realtors in our "B" Customer list. In large surveys, less than 5,000 people are used to represent the entire country. At a statistical level, any time the sample of people is more than 50, we know statistically the results will be more representative of the population.

In a population with more than one hundred members, a sample of 5% or 10% can be adequate. When the population number is small, for example 80 people, the larger the percentage drawn from the total the better. In this example, 25% of 80 is 20 interviews, 10 from our "A" customers, and 10 from our "B" customers.

In selecting the ten individuals to interview, you may want to consider other factors like gender, age, and time in the business. For example, if there are 60 women in the group of 80, we will need six women in each set of 10 people to interview.

## SELECTING A FOCUSED SAMPLE

In conducting a focused sample, you select those customers to interview that have essentially the same general characteristics. In our example, Realtors who are A and B customers are focus groups. That is, the A group customers are similar because they represent those customers that give you approximately 80% of your business and are likely your best and loyal customers. The B group customers are similar in that they give you significantly less business and they are likely sending significant business to your competitors. Additional examples of focused samples would be choosing Realtor customers who reside in specific geographic locations, lost Realtor customers, new Realtors, or Realtor customers who are in controlled business relationships.

If you were interested in sampling a larger customer group, for example a sample that would be representative of all of your customers, you would conduct interviews with a Random Sample that would cut across all your customer segments. To select the customers for a random sample, choose customers at random from your complete list of customers.

Sample sizes can vary depending upon the size of the particular segment you are interviewing, the total size of your customer base, or the total population in your market. In general, a sample size of between 10 and 20 percent of the customer group you are interviewing will be sufficient.

## INTERVIEW QUESTIONS

Interviewing customers is a lot like the game of Twenty Questions. In an interview, you ask a series of planned questions intended to obtain specific information. One of the key elements in effective customer interviewing is having a list of prepared questions. The best interviews are carefully planned. We have developed a Customer Interview Guide that lists potential questions for title customers.

We suggest using our CBA Customer Interview Guide as a starting point to develop your own interview questions. The questions are designed to explore a number of key areas with respect to customer needs and expectations.

In the CBA Customer Interview Guide you will find questions that focus on:

1. The professional background of the customer.
2. The structure of the customer's business and business needs.

3.  Business issues and barriers.

4.  Reasons for choosing a title company.

5.  Competitors.

6.  Technology proficiency.

7.  Communication preferences.

8.  Service and product preferences.

9.  Customer satisfaction.

10. Customer profile.

The questions you develop will need to be aligned with the customers you are interviewing. You do not want to make the mistake of asking a real estate lawyer, questions that are more suitable for a loan officer.

Before selecting or writing questions, you should determine who will do the interviews and how responses will be documented. In our experience, any experienced employee can learn to interview. In addition to your sales staff, you might have a manager, senior examiner, or your top escrow officer learn to conduct interviews. Generally, you want to match the level of your employee to the customer's level. For example, owners or management staff should interview owners and management, title and closing staff should interview real estate agents and loan processors, and so on. If possible, we recommend sending two people to each interview, one person to ask the questions and one person to act as a recorder, writing down the customer's answers.

Documenting the customer's responses is an important step and you will want to do it systematically. Recording answers does not need to be difficult, but you do want to be thorough. One simple technique is for the Recorder to take a blank tablet of paper and number the customer responses as the interview progresses.

Several years ago, it would be common for people to ask us if a tape recorder could be used to record customer responses. Our advice was "No" because our experience was the process made the customer nervous and it was not conducive to a natural free-flowing conversation. It was also more time consuming to transpose what was recorded after the interview. Today, the same question can be asked for the use of an electronic tablet, given the recorder has good electronic typing skills. The difference today is electronic downloads are efficient. Our best advice is to ask customers what makes them comfortable.

Following a systematic process will allow you later to return to what you have recorded, easily study and draw conclusions from what the customer said. If you are comparing results for a large number of customers you need to be sure you are comparing answers to the same question.

PRACTICE

The key to successful interviewing is preparing the questions ahead of time and practicing the full interview. Just like a professional actor, the good interviewer practices to eliminate poorly worded or badly stated questions, awkward pauses, and reading from notes. Poorly conducted interviews tell the customer you are unprofessional. An unprepared interviewer is wasting the customer's time.

Less experienced interviewers are encouraged to conduct several role-play practice sessions before actually interviewing a customer. The role-play should be conducted with three or four people. One person is the interviewer, one person the interviewee, one person a recorder, and one person observes the interview and provides detailed feedback regarding the interviewer's performance. A now classic excellent source book on interviewing techniques can be found in The Smart Interviewer, by Bradford Smart.[19]

The prepared interviewer knows the interview questions so well that he or she can easily maintain good eye contact without appearing to read from a script. Follow-up questions to each scripted question are important and they should be practiced as well. You will not be able to anticipate exactly the types of responses customers will make but in general follow-up questions

---

[19] Bradford D. Smart, *The Smart Interviewer* (New York: John Wiley & Sons, 1989).

are important for you to anticipate. Good follow-up questions add important detail, quantify or qualify a response, or seek examples from the customer. Consider the following interview sequence:

Interviewee:    It is important that we receive timely confirmation on scheduled closings.

Interviewer:    What types of communications would you like?

Interviewee:    Phone calls or E-mails are best. Most of our staff are equipped with some type of mobile device and are instructed to be in constant contact.

Interviewer:    What would be your first and second choices for electronic communications?

Interviewee:    Our first choice would actually be text messages when they are appropriate and efficient, next would come confirmation by e-mails.

The key to successful follow-up questions is active listening on the part of the interviewer. We encourage recorders to ask follow-up questions to engage in the interview and to seek clarification when needed. A recorder can always interject with "Could you elaborate on that?" There are two additional components of customer interviewing that you should practice:

1.  The opening. How you start the interview.

2.  The closing summary. How you end the interview.

107

When you meet someone for the first time, there is a natural period of chatting, where one gets to know the person. If you know the person, some social interaction is still important before getting started. The exception to this idea is if you know the customer would prefer to get right down to business. Once you begin the formal interview, we recommend a scripted introduction like the following. Here is an example that you can adapt to fit your needs. It begins after a few basic rapport-building interactions.

[Introduction]

We want to thank you for taking time to meet with us today. The purpose of our discussion is to determine how we can better assist you with your business needs. The interview will take about 45 minutes. (Insert name of employee) will be acting as a recorder today. He/she will be writing down what you tell us. I will be asking a set of prepared questions. As we go through the interview, please do not hesitate to ask us questions. In addition, if there is a question you do not want to talk about, please say so. Do you have any questions?

When you are finished with the interview, it is important to close out the interview on a positive note. Here is an example.

[Closing Summary]

[Customer Name]. We have come to the end of our interview. Do you have any final questions or comments for us, or are there any issues you would like to discuss that we have not covered? We want to thank you for your participation and taking the time to talk with us. We highly value your comments and insights and we look forward to working with you in the future. Thank you again.

## INTERVIEW SCHEDULE

In planning for or scheduling an interview, it is important to consider the setting where the interview will take place. The location of the interview needs to be quiet, free of distractions and comfortable. We do not recommend interviewing at lunch or after business hours. The last thing you want is having to pass the ketchup in the middle of an important question. You need to arrange for a space that is confidential, and where your recorder can easily write down customer responses. A table in a closing room is an example of a good interview space.

As a part of your scheduling process, you will need to send an introduction letter (e.g., attached to an e-mail) or phone the customer to explain the purpose of the interview, a suggested interview location, how the results of the interview will be used, and how long the interview will last.

Once the interview is scheduled, use a follow-up phone call or e-mail to confirm your interview date and answer any logistical questions. On the day before the interview is scheduled, send an e-mail reminder.

In your letter of introduction or phone script, explain the purpose of the interview, stress that you are interested in learning more about how you can better align your company to meet the business needs of the customer. Below is an example of the main body of an introduction you could provide in an e-mail letter or phone call. Use this example, as a starter you can customize to fit your needs.

> We are starting a new initiative to talk to key customers in our market. We would like to include you in our interviews. This interview will not be a sales call. We are interested in talking to you about your business and how we can provide the best service and value to you. We hope to use the results of our interview to add greater value to your business experience with us. The interview will take approximately 45 minutes and we would like to arrange a time and place that will be convenient for you. I will be bringing an associate with me to help with the interview. (Suggest a date and time or ask the customer to provide a date and time. Indicate that you will be following up to confirm the interview.)

AFTER EACH INTERVIEW

After the interview, you will need to go over what you learned. We call this a debriefing. It is a good idea for the interviewer and recorder to share what they have learned. There may be, for example, a particular question you want to modify in some manner or something that needs to be added. This is also a good time to discuss what went well in terms of the interview process and what could be improved for the next time. In terms of interview findings, there may be items the customer told you that you could act on immediately.

We recommend sending a follow-up thank you note to each customer. A personalized follow-up letter or e-mail to each customer is important. This letter should not read like a form letter.

You can further personalize your letter by highlighting a few of the things you learned from the customer and how you will follow-up. Consider the following example in writing your letter:

## EXAMPLE OF A THANK YOU LETTER

Date

Dear [Name];

Thank you for completing the interview with us on [date]. We appreciate the time and effort you took to tell us what is important to you including ideas on how we can work to improve our service to you. We believe talking to our customers to find out what they think is one of the most important things we can do.

We are looking forward to continuing to consult with you to seek your advice. (Insert any specific actions you will be taking for the customer that were mentioned during the interview.)

Please contact our sales representative or me if there are any additional immediate ways we can help to serve you better. We will be looking forward to our continuing relationship with you and assisting you with your business needs.

Sincerely, (Company owner or CEO\President.)

## ANALYZE FINDINGS

At the conclusion of each interview, the information collected needs to be memorialized. While the information is fresh it will be important to note impressions and nuances from the customer. This is also a good time for the interviewer and recorder to identify and fill in any missing information in the recorder's notes. Immediate actions that can be taken for a particular customer can also be noted.

Once all your interviews are completed, you should identify types of actions (tactics) you can take with individual customers as well as tactics for a customer group or specific customer segment. In combining results for a customer group, you are identifying characteristics and needs that are common and can be applied to the entire group in question. One simple analysis step to follow is to gather up and list side by side, all of the answers you received for each of your interview questions in order. For example, take all the answers you received from your interviews for question number one and combine them together, looking for common characteristics and similarities. Repeat this process for each of your interview questions.

The most challenging part of analyzing your interview findings is summarizing the information and interpreting the information in ways that will set you apart from your competitors. Your challenge is to identify customer needs and buying factors that you can directly translate into meaningful new sales strategies and tactics.

The following is a list of questions to use in analyzing and summarizing your customer interview results. As you summarize your findings from each of your interview questions, list your top four most frequent customer responses for each question. These questions can be used to analyze either individual customer responses or responses representative of an entire customer group or segment.

Analysis Questions:

1. What does this customer (or customer group) value the most?
2. What are the customer's top service needs?
3. What are the most significant ways you can help the customer improve their business?
4. What are their most frequent order-entry needs?
5. What are their most frequent title production needs?
6. What are their most frequent pre-closing needs?
7. What are their most frequent closing day needs?
8. What are their most frequent post-closing needs?
9. What are your competitors doing consistently that you are not?
10. Where does your service stand out as superior?
11. Where does your service fail?

12. What are the preferred types of communication?

13. What does the group expect from your website?

14. How can you interface with the technology, electronic communications and social networks the customer is using?

15. What does the group expect from your sales staff?

## INTEGRATE YOUR FINDINGS

The final step in the customer interview process is to incorporate your findings into your market and sales plans. This is where all your efforts in interviewing customers should pay off. The focus should be to identify the sales strategies and tactics that will lead to increased sales and eventual strategic advantage over your competitors.

## GUIDING PRINCIPLES FOR CHAPTER 7

1. Customer interviews are not designed to be sales calls, but they often result in an order.

2. Information unique to a customer will provide you with individual sales tactics. Information common to a group will provide you with a strategic advantage.

3. According to the 80/20 rule, 20% of your customers account for 80% of your income. Use the 80/20 rule and your customer A, B, and C customer rankings to help identify who you will interview.

4. In general, a sample size of between 10 and 20 percent of the customer group you are interviewing will be sufficient.

5. One of the key elements in effective customer interviewing is having a list of prepared questions.

6. Consider contacting CBA to learn more about the CBA Customer Interview Guide.

7. Any experienced employee can learn to interview.

8. Good follow-up questions add important detail, quantify or qualify a response or seek examples from the customer.

9. We do not recommend interviewing at lunch or after business hours.

10. Your challenge is to identify customer needs and buying factors you can directly translate into meaningful new sales strategies and tactics.

## DEVELOPMENT IDEAS\QUESTIONS FOR CHAPTER 7

1.  Meet with your management and sales teams to plan the customer interviewing process.

2.  Follow our planning steps outlined in this chapter.

3.  Challenge your staff to answer these two questions after each interview is completed:

    - What have we learned from the customer that will help us gain more business from that customer?

    - What have we learned that is an important idea, sales tactic or strategy for the customer segment the customer represents?

# CUSTOMER SATISFACTION
## CHAPTER 8

This chapter focuses on customer satisfaction and developing a satisfaction survey. We have included the topic of customer satisfaction and measuring satisfaction because we believe that feedback from customers about our products and services must be a part of the formula that guides our future actions. It is an essential part of being customer focused and market-driven. Satisfied customers come back. Repeat customers become loyal customers. Loyal customer spread the word. Customer loyalty is shaped by a customer's experiences and his/her satisfaction with those experiences. To increase a customer's loyalty we must work to increase a customer's level of satisfaction over time.

One of the difficulties in assessing customer satisfaction is knowing what is the best measure of satisfaction. For most business owners the fact that he/she is making money and some customers are returning is evidence that customers are satisfied. Unfortunately, we know that using a company is not evidence of satisfaction.

Customer revenue, orders over time (retention), and share of business (the amount of business the customer gives you as opposed to other companies) all are indirect measures of satisfaction. They are necessary but not sufficient. Other anecdotal indicators of satisfaction include when your customer refers you to other customers or when your customer refers to your company as "My Title Company."

Consider for a moment if you were asked to rate your satisfaction with your doctor, dentist, dry cleaner, grocery, or local coffee shop. Many Americans use the same doctor or dentist and yet when asked will say they do not like or trust their doctor. Roger has been going to the same dry cleaner for twenty-two years because they are convenient, yet in all that time, they have never greeted him by name or shown the least interest in his business. He would leave that business tomorrow if another were as convenient. If you own a title agency, you would welcome a Realtor who uses you because you are convenient, however, there is no reason to believe that the customer is loyal or satisfied just because they use you.

Today, given the number of reality television shows like Restaurant Impossible and Kitchen Nightmares that show failing businesses, we know that a business that does not change and stops listening to customers is doomed. If you want to know what customers are feeling about your products and services, you have to ask.

The most direct and perhaps best measure of satisfaction is asking the customer. For example, using a survey, we could ask, How did we do? How was our service? How satisfied are you?"

These are direct questions about satisfaction. The problem is interpreting the answer depends on the way we asked the questions (demands), the questions we ask (content), who we asked (audience), how many people we ask (sample size), the scale or choice of answers we provide, and the way we interpret the results.

## DEMAND

Most of us have experienced a survey in which we were asked our satisfaction by the person we are evaluating. "How was dinner?" Psychologists[20] in the 1960s demonstrated that placing demands on the person doing the evaluation changed their answer. Many of us have had the experience when a car sales person asks us to provide a favorable survey rating at the conclusion of a new car sale. Telling us his bonus or job depends on our rating.

If you are going to measure customer satisfaction in a survey you have to be sure the customer is under no pressure (demand) to give you a favorable evaluation. We want the customer to be honest and objective. We want the customer to feel no pressure to provide a positive rating. We want to know how they feel or felt at the time of service.

A second dimension of demand is how the survey is delivered. We can ask in-person, we can ask on the telephone, we

---

[20] Robert Rosenthal and Ralph L. Rosenthal, *Artifacts in Behavioral Research* (Classic Books, Oxford University Press, 2009).

119

can have the person fill out a card in the office, we can send a survey in the mail, we can e-mail a survey, or the survey can be taken on-line. Each method has a strength and each method has its problems. The number one problem being getting the customer to complete the survey.

A third dimension that has demand characteristics is the timing of the survey and the frequency with which a customer is surveyed. If you ask a customer about a closing that happened that day you will get a different result than if you ask a day later or a month later. Likewise, if you ask a person to complete a survey and then send four reminders you are placing demands on the customer that will affect the results.

AUDIENCE

If you own a title insurance agency, the types of customers you might survey regarding their satisfaction with your closing services might include: buyers, sellers, Realtors, Attorneys, lenders, and developers. The question might be where to start or who to exclude. Twenty years ago, when we introduced the idea of customer surveys to title insurance managers, the target audience in most residential markets were the listing Realtors. The reasoning was the seller ordered the title work, the listing Realtor picked the title company for the seller, and it was the Realtor who was the real customer. Today with the internet and social networking, you would be wise to survey each customer who was at the table.

## CONTENT

The questions you ask depend on the audience and they depend on what information you are trying to gather. In developing content (questions) we have to consider the audience and how much information or specificity we need in the question. Different customer segments have different needs or issues, survey content should be designed to gain different input from different customers. A lender may be more concerned about specific escrow processing services and communications regarding the lending package. An attorney may have specific needs regarding the production of the title commitment. A Realtor will likely be interested in the locations of your offices and the appearance of your reception and closing areas. A buyer or seller will be interested in how the title company helped them understand the closing process and what the title policy insures.

Most surveys do have some questions that are intended for all customers. For example:

On a scale of 1 to 5 with 5 being Very Satisfied, rate your overall satisfaction with our company.

The difficulty is determining what a "3" means to an attorney, lender, Realtor, and buyer. As a rule of thumb, if you have three types of customers, ask different (specific) questions for each of the three types. Likewise, if your service has three features, ask the customer to evaluate his/her satisfaction with each feature and then evaluate your service or company overall. For example, of a buyer:

1. Rate your satisfaction with the way you were received.
2. Rate your satisfaction with your closer.
3. Rate your satisfaction with the closing experience.
4. Rate your satisfaction with our company overall.

Before leaving content, it is important to understand the mechanics of defining what you want evaluated. Note in the examples below, we better define what each feature is and what behavior is expected, i.e., what is being evaluated in each one.

1. Rate your satisfaction with our location, parking, the building, common areas, and restrooms.
2. Rate your satisfaction with the way you were greeted and received by our receptionist (or other employees) in the lobby. Were you satisfied that your reception was polite, friendly, and courteous?

3. Rate your satisfaction working with our title, department: documents accurate and timely. People: professional, polite, positive.

4. Rate your satisfaction with your closer: prepared, professional, polite, positive.

5. Rate your satisfaction with the closing experience: Start time, closing room, and length of the closing.

6. Rate your satisfaction with our company overall.

Good survey questions ask you to evaluate one thing and one thing only. In the first example below, we only ask the person to evaluate politeness. In the second example, we add other features we want evaluated. The problem is, the customer might be satisfied with the closers' warmth, but not her politeness. If you want to know about each feature, ask a separate question.

1. Rate your satisfaction with the politeness of our closer.

2. Rate your satisfaction with the politeness, friendliness, positive can-do attitude, and warmth of our closer.

Before leaving this example, notice in question number one above, you might use a different rating scale. For example, you might ask the customer to rate his/her agreement with the statement:

1. Our closer was very polite.

When the content question is worded this way we are looking for strong agreement or disagreement (a different scale). Using different scales in a survey is acceptable and may be a good practice, but you have to be careful you know how you will use the results later. If you plan to add up all the results and give one score, you should ask all the questions in the same way and you cannot use different scales.

Consider the examples below:

1. Rate your satisfaction with the politeness of our closer on a five-point scale...
2. Were you satisfied with the politeness of our closer? Rate your satisfaction on a five-point scale...

The wording of the first question is our standard wording. The wording in the second question really demands a yes or no answer. Because of the tricky way the question is worded, it will drive (demand) a rating of "4." Improper demand can also be created by telling the customer what rating you expect. For example:

We hope you were very satisfied with our closer? We are committed to your satisfaction. Rate your satisfaction on a five-point scale…

A properly worded question is neutral, asks for one feature to be evaluated, and uses an appropriate scale. For example:

1.  Rate your satisfaction with our closer on a five-point scale with 1 being Very Dissatisfied and 5 being Very Satisfied.

## SCALE

Surveys and questionnaires are designed to assess a person's thoughts and feelings about a product or service. For example, I could ask a person, "Is title insurance important to have on a residential transaction?" If the answer is either "No" or "Yes," we say that the question's content is bi-polar or has two answers at either end of a continuum. If the answer is either "No," "Maybe," or "Yes," we have a question requiring a three-point scale: "No," "Neither No or Yes," or "Yes."

The answers to some questions can be scaled, but the scale does not have an absolute end point (i.e., No or Yes). For example, if we asked a customer "How hot do you like your chili?" The person could answer from "Not hot at all" to "Take me to the hospital." In this example the scale could be from 1 (not hot) to 5 (very Hot), but given the nature of chili the scale will be insensitive to what is being measured. For Chili, we use the Scoville scale, which goes from 0 to 2,000,000 units of heat.

For our purposes, we recommend using a Likert scale. The Likert scale is named after psychologist Rensis Likert. The Likert Scale is a symmetric or "balanced" measure because there are equal numbers of positive and negative positions. The seven point Likert scale below measures a person's agreement on a seven-point scale.

1 = Strongly Disagree

2 = Disagree

3 = Somewhat (slightly) Disagree

4 = Neither Disagree or Agree

5 = Somewhat (slightly) Agree

6 = Agree

7 = Strongly Agree

Research has demonstrated that consistent results occur using either a five point or seven point Likert scale. For practical reasons we recommend the five-point Likert scale. Technically, the items in a survey are called the Likert items and the score derived after the survey is completed is the Likert Scale Score.

In the example below, we have drawn a line down the middle of the scale. In the early days of surveying you would total the number of 1 (0), 2 (1), 3 (2), 4 (5), and 5 (2). If you total all the ratings, the sum is 38. This sum when divided by the number of items (10) gives you the person's average Likert score = 3.8.

## EXAMPLE OF A CLOSING SURVEY USING A LIKERT SCALE

Rate your disagreement or agreement with each statement
using the five-point scale below, rate each item:

| Strongly Disagree | Disagree | Neutral | Agree | Strongly Agree |
|---|---|---|---|---|
| 1 ☐ | 2 ☐ | 3 ☐ | 4 ☐ | 5 ☐ |

1. Our building has convenient parking.

| 1 ☐ | 2 ☐ | 3 ☐ | 4 ■ | 5 ☐ |
|---|---|---|---|---|

2. The building, common areas, and restrooms were attractive and clean.

| 1 ☐ | 2 ☐ | 3 ☐ | 4 ☐ | 5 ■ |
|---|---|---|---|---|

3. Our receptionist was welcoming (polite, friendly, and courteous).

| 1 ☐ | 2 ☐ | 3 ☐ | 4 ■ | 5 ☐ |
|---|---|---|---|---|

4. The title department provided you with accurate documents.

| 1 ☐ | 2 ■ | 3 ☐ | 4 ☐ | 5 ☐ |
|---|---|---|---|---|

5. Your documents were delivered on time.

| 1 ☐ | 2 ☐ | 3 ☐ | 4 ■ | 5 ☐ |
|---|---|---|---|---|

6. Your closer was prepared.

| 1 ☐ | 2 ☐ | 3 ■ | 4 ☐ | 5 ☐ |
|---|---|---|---|---|

7. Your closing was on time and length of time to close was as promised.

| 1 ☐ | 2 ☐ | 3 ■ | 4 ☐ | 5 ☐ |
|---|---|---|---|---|

8. All of your questions were answered.

| 1 ☐ | 2 ☐ | 3 ☐ | 4 ■ | 5 ☐ |
|---|---|---|---|---|

9. You were very satisfied with your experience at our company.

| 1 ☐ | 2 ☐ | 3 ☐ | 4 ■ | 5 ☐ |
|---|---|---|---|---|

10. You would highly recommend our company to others.

| 1 ☐ | 2 ☐ | 3 ☐ | 4 ☐ | 5 ■ |
|---|---|---|---|---|

## EXAMPLE OF A CLOSING SURVEY USING A LIKERT SCALE

Rate your disagreement or agreement with each statement
using the five-point scale below, rate each item:

| Strongly Disagree | Disagree | Neutral | Agree | Strongly Agree |
|---|---|---|---|---|
| 1 ☐ | 2 ☐ | 3 ☐ | 4 ☐ | 5 ☐ |

1. Our building has convenient parking.

1 ☐   2 ☐   3 ☐   4 ☐   5 ☐

2. The building, common areas, and restrooms were attractive and clean.

1 ☐   2 ☐   3 ☐   4 ☐   5 ☐

3. Our receptionist was welcoming (polite, friendly, and courteous).

1 ☐   2 ☐   3 ☐   4 ☐   5 ☐

4. The title department provided you with accurate documents.

1 ☐   2 ☐   3 ☐   4 ☐   5 ☐

5. Your documents were delivered on time.

1 ☐   2 ☐   3 ☐   4 ☐   5 ☐

6. Your closer was prepared.

1 ☐   2 ☐   3 ☐   4 ☐   5 ☐

7. Your closing was on time and length of time to close was as promised.

1 ☐   2 ☐   3 ☐   4 ☐   5 ☐

8. All of your questions were answered.

1 ☐   2 ☐   3 ☐   4 ☐   5 ☐

9. You were very satisfied with your experience at our company.

1 ☐   2 ☐   3 ☐   4 ☐   5 ☐

10. You would highly recommend our company to others.

1 ☐   2 ☐   3 ☐   4 ☐   5 ☐

Today online programs will calculate a score for you, but you must remember that all the items have to be worded to use the same scale. Look at the two items below. Both statements can be rated using our Likert scale except the items are the opposite.

1. Our building has ample and convenient parking.
2. Our building needs more convenient parking.

For Item 1, a rating of 4 is positive. For Item 2, a rating of 4 is negative. When you word items differently, you have to introduce the appropriate scale. Unless you are experienced in survey research, you should use one scale and make sure all the items are worded for that scale.

Before leaving the topic of scales, we are going to repeat that a Likert scale is anchored and balanced. It has the opposites on each end of the scale and the same number of negative as positive points on the scale. Consider the scale in the example below:

Improper Scale

1 = Very Dissatisfied

2 = Dissatisfied

3 = Slightly Satisfied

4 = Satisfied

5 = Sort of Satisfied

6 = Happy

7 = Very Satisfied

This scale was used in a survey, we saw. Unfortunately, we couldn't stop the survey before it was released. As you can see, the scale has several technical problems. First, there is no neutral point or midpoint, so it is unbalanced. Second, the labels used for each number are not ordinal. You can't go from Satisfied to sort of satisfied and the word "Happy" should not be on the scale. In this example, the designer was trying to give the rater more options, but in doing so violated the rules of survey design.

SAMPLE SIZE

In our chapter on Customer Interviews we discussed the concept of sample size when performing customer interviews and analyzing the results. If you will be using your survey results as a representative indicator of satisfaction levels for a group of customers you serve, sample size is important to consider. For example, if you call on 50 different Realtor customers and receive surveys back from 10 of them, you will have a 20 percent sample, which is more than adequate. Refer to our discussions on selecting customers to interview and selecting a focused sample for more information on sample size.

## MECHANICS

There are a number of additional factors to consider in determining when and how to administer a survey, including, your reasons for administering the survey, the period of time the survey will cover, the communications to the customer you use to provide a rationale, and user instructions. You will also have to consider whether you want to survey satisfaction for the latest transaction, or for a longer period of time, for example, the calendar year. Customer annoyance is also an issue. You have to be careful not to give out too many surveys to the same customer.

## BUILDING YOUR SURVEY

There are several national on-line vendors, for example Survey Monkey, that offer survey design and administration services that make it easy to conduct a survey and still protect the customer's anonymity. Our advice is to use one of these services and stick to professional surveys and items. Whatever you decide, the customers selected to survey should not be chosen by the employees most affected by the survey and the survey should never be filled out with an employee or manager present.

## GUIDING PRINCIPLES FOR CHAPTER 8

1. To increase a customer's loyalty we must work to increase each customer's level of satisfaction and sustain that level over time.

2. If you want to know what customers are feeling about your products and services, you have to ask.

3. Consider whether you want to survey satisfaction for the latest transaction, or for a longer period of time.

4. Often the satisfaction issues a lender has are different from those of a Realtor, Attorney or Builder. Design survey items to match the service and need\value expectations of your different customer groups.

5. A properly worded question is neutral, asks for one feature to be evaluated, and uses an appropriate scale.

6. Research has demonstrated that consistent results occur using either a five point or seven point Likert scale.

7. If you will be using your survey results as a representative indicator of satisfaction levels for a group of customers you serve, sample size is important to consider.

8. In developing a survey to implement there are a number of logistical issues to consider including the goals of the survey, the period of time the survey will cover, the communications you provide to users, and how frequently you administer the survey to the same customer.

## DEVELOPMENT IDEAS\QUESTIONS FOR CHAPTER 8

1. Develop a customer satisfaction survey and process for your company.

2. Track the results and ratings from your survey quarterly, or at six-month intervals, to evaluate what improvements are necessary for your company.

3. Ask your sales team to consider how survey findings can be integrated with sales strategies and tactics?

4. Use the results of your survey process to improve operations, including leadership and management.

# SALES SKILLS

## CHAPTER 9

A sales manager once told us that he did not know exactly what his most successful sales person did, but he was convinced he had an innate ability to sell. Meaning he was a "born" salesman. Our bet is that if the sales manager had taken the time to study his top performer, he would have identified a set of basic sales skills that are common to most good sales people. In our thinking, selling is a skill or set of skills that can be taught.

When you Google the words "sales skills" a long list of references immediately appears beginning with Dale Carnegie. Carnegie's courses on self-improvement, salesmanship, corporate training, public speaking, and interpersonal skills starting in 1922 were instrumental in the American approach to selling.

Roger reports that his grandfather (who was a great sales person) took a Dale Carnegie course on public speaking and human relationships in the 1930s. In 1970, Dale Carnegie's *How to Win Friends and Influence People*[21]" was the text in a course offered in Roger's graduate Psychology program. *How to Win Friends and Influence People* has gone through many editions and reissues and today there is a new version entitled, *How to Win Friends and Influence*

---

[21] Dale Carnegie, *How To Win Friends And Influence People* (Simon and Schuster, New York, 1936).

*People in the Digital Age.*[22] The premise of this text is even in the digital age, the interpersonal and relationship skills, written about by Dale Carnegie are still relevant. In our opinion, they are essential.

Selling is about building trust and creating relationships. It is using words and actions to influence what people do. Ever since Dale Carnegie, academics and sales experts have written extensively about the skills needed for successful sales. As business consultants and authors, we have never thought of ourselves as pure sales people but over the years, we have worked with many successful sales people and learned from them.

In this chapter and Chapter 10, rather than cover the complete gamut of skills often covered in a general course on sales, we have selected a few key skills we believe are essential for successful business-to-business sales. These skills include: initial presentations, asking planned and structured questions, relationship development, consultative or solutions based selling, sales call planning, expense tracking and customer profile development.

## FIRST IMPRESSIONS

Research has shown that people can form a "first impression" very quickly, in seconds, and these impressions can

---

[22] Dale Carnegie and Associates, *How to Win Friends and Influence People in the Digital Age.* (Simon & Schuster, New York, 2012).

remain for long periods whether accurate or not. We also know first impressions can be misleading. The way a person is dressed, their height and physical appearance, their attractiveness, and the way they speak all have an immediate effect that can be misleading.

As a sales person, the question you need to answer is what impression do you want to give or leave with the customer and are you doing everything to give that impression. The other day, Roger had an appointment with a new doctor. The office decor was expensive furniture and oriental rugs. The office brochure had a picture of four doctors all in suits and white lab coats. Needless to say, Roger was surprised when his doctor walked into the examining room wearing jeans, a sweater, and tennis shoes. He did not seem like a doctor. He was wearing almost the same thing Roger was wearing. However, when it came to the exam and discussing why Roger was there, he was very professional and personable. Later in the back office Roger could hear the doctor joking with the staff and having fun. He seemed like a great boss.

One of the first jobs Chris had in his college years was working in a ski shop at a resort in Western New York. Chris often stood at the front counter and attempted to engage people as they entered the shop. Chris, who is a great skier and has many friends is not naturally outgoing and at that time knew little about creating a good first impression.

Eventually, the shop manager realized when Chris worked the front counter sales were down. In fact, customers commented on Chris' quiet demeanor and often mistook his behavior as uninterested or standoffish. Before too long Chris was sent behind the showroom doors to the repair shop where he was far removed from customer contact. His demotion proved insightful and affected the way Chris interacts with strangers. The simple lesson Chris learned was customers are more likely to buy if they are engaging with you. Creating a positive first impression and engaging the customer act as a gateway to developing relationships and sales.

In Chapter 6, we emphasized the importance of matching the sales person's style with the style of the customer. The problem is when you first meet a person, you may not know his/her style, therefore, what matters most is the impression you give. That is, the way you engage the customer and get to know the customer.

If possible, first contacts and first visits with the customer should be carefully planned. If you know beforehand the customer has good social and verbal skills and is generally warm and accepting, you can plan to engage the customer initially with a few minutes of social banter. If on the other hand, you know the customer is more results oriented and likes to get right down to business, you can quickly get to the point of asking planned questions. In general, a sales person needs to respect the customers time, carefully listen, ask good questions, act courteously, and use the time with the customer wisely.

In *How to Win Friends and Influence People*, Carnegie discusses "Six Ways to Make People Like You." The six ways are:

1. Become genuinely interested in other people.
2. Smile.
3. Use the person's name.
4. Be a good listener.
5. Talk in terms of the other person's interest.
6. Make the other person feel important – and do it sincerely.

Many people learn these skills early in their life, so we think of them as naturally friendly. What Dale Carnegie did was teach us these are skills that can be practiced and improved.

For example, Roger Lubeck is a curious person. He is interested in how things work and why. He likes literature, history, biology, physics, and computers. However, he isn't mechanical. Since he was ten he has been interested in why people do what they do and what makes people different. Whatever the origins of his curiosity, Roger became a Psychologist in part because of his curiosity. Now, when he meets a stranger, he might ask any of the following questions:

1. What do you do for work?
2. How long have you done it?

3. Where did you go to school?

4. How much education do you have?

5. Do you have a family?

6. Where do you live?

7. Do you have any hobbies or other interests?

8. Where do you go on vacation?

9. What cities, foods, music, or literature do you like?

10. What do you like best and worst about your work?

He asks questions like these to get to know the person. If asked he talks about himself. In fact, he has a prepared speech about his life, his company, his books, his job, and his values. One of the surprising things Roger does not do is judge the other person's style too quickly. He usually likes to interact and observe a person in several different situations. For example, a business owner can be clear and decisive in a one-on-one meeting and vague and uncertain in a group meeting.

The next time you meet a person for the first time, examine what do you do and what questions you ask? What do you learn about the person? What questions went unasked? Just like Roger's list of questions, make your own list of twenty questions and next time make sure you ask most of the questions on your list.

## PLANNED QUESTIONS

The initial first contacts a sales person makes with the customer, and the service the title company provides, acts as the foundation for the customer relationship that develops. A large part of any strong relationship is trust and trust takes time to develop. Trust does not happen overnight. Following through in a timely manner on what was promised and doing what you say you will do goes a long way to cement early relationships. Before the first meetings with the customer, sales staff should research as much as they can about the customer and the customer's company. This activity should include studying company websites and any written material available.

In Chapter 7, we said that one of the keys to determining what customer's value is simply asking the right questions. The types of structured customer interviews we recommend are not sales calls, but they often lead to sales. In fact, we recommend that production and management staff take part in structured customer interviews when they can. Customers often tell us they are impressed with the title agency has taken the time to discuss details on improving the customer's business. Ultimately, all good, intelligent questions have the possibility of turning up sales opportunities.

When sales staff first make sales calls with customers, we recommend planning the types of questions to ask. Asking the right questions will increase credibility, but asking the wrong questions or too many will not be effective. If structured customer interviews have taken place prior to the initial sales calls, consider those results in planning the next series of questions. Also, review your sales plan and the objectives and sales tactics planned for the specific customer segment the customer represents.

In planning your sales questions, follow this strategy: design your questions to follow a natural progression from fact-based questions to more open-ended questions and discussion, ending with questions that are specific to your products and services.

The progression from specific to open-ended and back to specific targeted discussion allows you to shape the discussion in a focused way but also allows the customer to expound on what is important to them. The following four types of sales questions to use in sequence are suggested by Thomas Freese[23]: Status questions; Issue questions; Implication questions; and, Solution questions.

## STATUS QUESTIONS

Status questions target specific information about the customer. Status questions are narrow in focus. Status questions

---

[23] Thomas A. Freese, *Secrets of Question Based Selling: How the Most Powerful Tool in Business Can Double your Sales Results* (Naperville, Illinois: Source Books, Inc. 2003), pp. 132-146.

help to control the conversation because of their specificity, but they also are relatively easy for the customer to discuss and thus a good starting point. Here are several examples.

1. What order entry process do you prefer with title companies?
2. Do you have a web site?
3. What percent of your customers would you say are local?
4. What percent of your customers find out about you online?

With new customers in particular, status questions are good for introducing your credibility, especially when you demonstrate in the questions you have done your research about the customer or the company.

1. I know that technology is important to you. What new technology are you using with your customers?
2. I know you use LinkedIn and Twitter quite frequently to drive people to your website. Have you found those methods beneficial in attracting new referrals to your business?

Status questions, provide an immediate focal point to shape the conversation, but the idea is to transition from the status statements quickly to more open-ended Issue questions.

143

## ISSUE QUESTIONS

Issue Questions allow the customer to expand on a topic. These questions encourage the customer to talk freely and expand on issues that are important to them. Compared to Status Questions, Issue Questions are open-ended.

1. What problems have you had in working with a title company?
2. You mentioned using LinkedIn and Twitter in your social networking. We do too. Have you been able to assess the effectiveness of this technology?
3. What issues have you had in tracking how successful these social networking methods are?

## IMPLICATION QUESTIONS

Implication Questions can be open-ended or more specific depending upon the further clarifications needed. The idea is to further expand on and probe the issues the customer identifies. You use Implication questions to understand why the particular issue identified is important to the customer. Here are two examples:

1. You said that timely order status updates are important. Can you give me an example of when and how that has been an issue and what happened?

2. You said that evaluating social networking activity based on the number of new referrals you receive is not the best way to evaluate your networking activity. What types of results are you looking for that would point to success?

## SOLUTION QUESTIONS

Solution Questions are traditionally used to close a sale. In posing solution questions your aim is to define your value to the customer. In following the progression from status questions through to possible solutions, it is important to move slowly. Remember, you are using a series of questions to probe possible customer needs and what the customer values. At each stage in this questioning process, follow-up questions to probe customer responses are important and the very best advice is to listen more than you talk. Your goal is to discover customer needs for which you can add value. Solution questions and suggestions should follow after you have demonstrated that you have listened and clearly heard what the customer has expressed as important needs. Here are examples:

1. Our order processing system automatically sends customers order status updates. As the closing date draws closer, the frequency of updates increases. Would that type of consistent service be important to you?

2.  We are tracking the number of new people that view our profile on LinkedIn each week along with several other tracking methods of customer contact on our website. I can arrange to show you several examples of our social networking tracking methods that may be applicable for you as well. Would you be interested?

## RELATIONSHIP DEVELOPMENT

Relationship selling on the part of sales staff for a long time has been associated with activities production personnel see as suspect at best. When we have asked title and escrow production staff what sales people do, the answer more often than not is play golf and take people out to lunch.

Although relationship development can play a key role in sales, what seems to have shifted in recent years is the emphasis on relationship development as the single most important skill in the sales person's tool bag. In research conducted by Dixon and Adamson, they found that only seven percent of the most successful sales people they studied had a relationship builder profile.[24] Other leading business authors agree:

"...the real meat of the relationship is when your customers see you as important to improving their business....the more you

---

[24] M. Dixon and B. Adamson, *The Challenger Sale: Taking Control of the Customer Conversation* (New York: The Penguin Group, 2011), pp.24.

ask good questions to uncover problems and needs and give good advice to solve problems and achieve customer goals, the more the customer will see you as a valuable resource."[25]

Our own findings in helping title insurance agents interview customers often reveal customers appreciate being taken out to dinner, or a good ticket to a sporting event, but they value more, sales people and companies that can offer sound business advice and help. We have often observed that escrow or title production employees who have the skills to switch to dedicated sales roles often are very successful because they bring a high level of technical advice and knowledge to the table that customers appreciate.

Neil Rackham, a leading business author writes:

"I believe that a customer relationship is the result and not the cause of successful selling. If you help people think differently and bring them new ideas, then you earn the right to a relationship."[26]

Nonetheless, strong customer relationships have been developed by companies where the employees have gotten to know customers extremely well and where the interaction and service is

---

[25] B. Tracy and M. Tracy, *Unlimited Sales Success: 12 Simple Steps for Selling More Than You Ever Thought Possible* (New York:: American Management Association, 2014), pp. 80-81.

[26] Rackman's comments can be found in a Foreword by him in: M. Dixon and B. Adamson, *The Challenger Sale: Taking Control of the Customer Conversation* (New York: The Penguin Group, 2011), pp. XV.

customized and personalized. What needs to be emphasized, however is that it is not just the sales person who is responsible for the customer relations. Building strong, long term relationships with customers is aided when a concentrated effort on the part of all employees and management is made to service the customer and know customer likes and dislikes, and what the customer values.

It is not just one factor that contributes to developing strong customer relationships, but a combination of factors that are ultimately important. Customer value and eventually trust and loyalty are driven by a combination of:

1. The products and services you provide.
2. How you deliver products and services.
3. Your company's performance.
4. Employee relationships, and
5. How the customer feels.

We were reminded of the multi-faceted nature of relationship development by a Title agent we worked with in Texas. We had just completed a production workflow-redesign project for both title and escrow operations, which included a major re-modeling of the reception and closing areas. About two months after the project was completed, a builder who did some business with the agent stopped by to congratulate the owners on the changes that had taken place. The builder said that he had enjoyed working with the employees of the title company in the past and appreciated their efforts, but the added benefit now was that the appearance of the office and especially the services available in the reception area reminded him of the same type of environment they had created in their sales offices. He said the new space reminded him of walking into their offices and he thought his customers would feel that same emotion. In fact, he said his customers would see the title company as an extension of his operations when they walked in through the front door. The builder then promised the owner he would send more business their way.

Emotions often do play a big role in the customer's decision to buy and many customers want to feel that your company in a way represents an extension of their company or you are "family." When a customer says that your company is "their title company," you know you have reached an important emotional threshold. In general, customers want to feel appreciated, comfortable, relaxed, respected, happy, and welcome in their interactions with you.

Sales staff can use a number of tactics that will help foster relationship development. Here is a list of relationship development activities we have observed sales staff use successfully with their customers:

1. Provide the customer with information about industry trends or best practices.

149

2. Invite them to an event related to one of their interests.

3. Invite them to attend a local charity event with you.

4. Invite them to a sales staff or production meeting and have them discuss their business.

5. Ask for their advice and act on it.

6. Whenever you can, use the word "We."

7. Take a picture of the customer, frame it and send with a personal note.

8. Give them your cell phone number.

9. Show them the latest App that has impressed you.

10. Offer assistance to help with one of their customers.

11. Ask them to call you personally when they have a problem.

12. Invite them to a fun event in your office.

13. Hand-deliver commitments.

14. Give them a professional referral you trust.

15. Give them a referral for your favorite: restaurant; travel agent; web site; hotel in another city; wine; fishing hole, golf course, or ski resort.

## CONSULTATIVE SELLING

As business consultants, we have long known what we really do best is provide ideas. A friend and mentor of ours once told us that developing procedures and protocols have their place, as does training, but what really gains the interest of the customer is to give them a good idea.

To discover what ideas might be of value to customers, our strategy is to step back and look at the bigger picture. We first examine the customer's organization to determine its many parts and then check alignment to evaluate how well they are integrated. In essence, we look for, what to improve by examining all the different components and systems that make up the company or organization.

For example, we might see that the major goals the leaders of the company have established need better understanding by line managers. The idea we sell is the need for better alignment between what the leaders of the company communicate as goals and what line managers actually put into practice. We then suggest ways for leadership to provide better communications to managers and new procedures to monitor performance and manage accountability.

You can approach the customers you target for title and escrow sales in similar ways. Here are three ways to discover ideas and sell like a consultant:

Look for how your title products and escrow services can be better aligned or integrated with the components of your customer's company. For example, if you are working with a Realtor, examine the ways the Realtor helps potential homebuyers determine title and closing costs remotely in the field when viewing a property. Suggest new ways to interface electronically with you to gain the needed information.

Look for how the delivery of your title and escrow products can match up better with your customer's systems. For example, if you are working with a loan officer, look at their communication systems to discover how you might improve the conveniences they experience when placing orders or check closing processing progress.

Examine your own systems and business components to see what could be of benefit for your customer to use or adapt in some way. For example, if you are working with an attorney, look to see how they receive the latest compliance and government regulatory information and how you might deliver to them and discuss, the same regulatory information you routinely receive.

A good strategy to discover important ideas is to get into the shoes of your customer. Spend a day with your customer in his or her business. Study the customer's service delivery workflow from start to finish. Interview key employees in your customer's business. Talk to your customer's customers to discover the issues they deal with.

Working as consultants, we often provide a comprehensive evaluation of a company's business. As a title professional, you may not be in the position to evaluate all of a company's business components, but there are many for which your advice and assistance would be helpful. If you do not have the needed expertise to evaluate a business component, look to see whom in your company would have that expertise. Offer this type of evaluation as a way to learn about your customer's business and provide new value-added ideas.

For example, who in your company can act as a consultant for marketing and sales plan development for your customer? Who can offer Business Plan help? Who can offer advice on technology? The advice you provide may be an added benefit and a distinct advantage over what your competition is providing. It will also be a significant way for you to differentiate your company and you as a salesperson.

## LOVING SALES

Terry Brown began a career in real estate with Burton Abstract & Title Company in Detroit Michigan in 1969. In 1983, Terry joined Ken Lingenfelter at Metropolitan Title as a partner and Senior Vice President. In the 1990s, Terry helped formulate Metropolitan's vision, to become "America's Premier Title Agency & Settlement Service Company." Later, as President of Metropolitan Title, Terry helped to encourage and inspire the growth of the sales team, the management team, and the leadership team. When Metropolitan was purchased by First American Title

Insurance Company in 2003, Terry stepped down as President, but stayed on in a key leadership and client relationship role.

Today Terry also serves as a business coach, leadership coach, sales coach and personal development coach! Terry says, "Helping and inspiring businesses and individuals to be the very best they can be is his passion!" According to Terry, a sales person has to make the shift from fear to love. What follows are Terry's Ten Principles for Loving Sales.

Terry Brown's principles for "LOVING-SALES"

1. Be yourself, but... be the very best version of yourself.
2. Work as hard on yourself as you do on your job!
3. Represent a quality company with a great culture and a great team and with high-value products and/or services.
4. Believe in yourself and in the products, services, and company you represent.
5. Only offer your services to those that need or want them.
6. Discover this by asking the <u>best questions</u> and truly listening, open-heartedly, to see if there is a genuine need or want for the things you offer.
7. Understand your prospect: deeply, genuinely, sincerely, and fully. This is where the "magic" happens. And, the "magic" is...trust.

8. Let them know you <u>understand</u> them. Become excellent at providing "feed-back" to them in the form of an articulate, succinct summary of their most pressing wants and needs. Practice and get good at summarizing their wants and needs.

9. If you are able to provide them truly with a product or service that will help satisfy a need or solve a problem, in sincerity, show them how…and offer it to them. If you have established <u>high trust</u>…and if you have a product or service that truly helps them…the rest is simple.

10. Where is the Love? In Terry's philosophy of selling, you have to love your company, love your team, love your product and services and love your prospects. And most importantly, cultivate a true desire to deeply <u>understand</u> each individual prospect and customer. To Love is to Understand and to understand is to love.

Terry believes that a sales person must deeply understand each individual prospect; their unique story, needs, wants, goals, fears, priorities and objectives.

## ASKING FOR THE ORDER

Jack Rogers was born in Illinois, but he sounds and acts like he was born in Texas. Jack has worked in the title business in San Antonio, Texas for nearly forty years. After twenty years owning his own title agency, Jack is now working in the commercial department for First American Title Company in San Antonio. When we asked Jack about his success at landing commercial deals in Texas, here were his guiding principles.

1. Prepare for your call.
2. Make sure you are talking to the decision maker.
3. Ask for the order.
4. Do not be afraid to ask for the big deal.
5. Never leave without asking for the order.
6. Add value. Sales representatives have to add value to the customer by referring business or other customers.

In talking about the importance of always asking for the order, Jack reminds us that the rules are changing. Brokers do not control the placement of title business as they once did. Their clients now have title company relationships.

## GUIDING PRINCIPLES FOR CHAPTER 9

1. Selling is a skill or set of skills that can be taught.

2. If possible, first contacts and first visits with the customer should be carefully planned.

3. All good, intelligent questions have the possibility of turning up sales opportunities.

4. Sequence your questions by progressing from specific to open-ended and back to specific targeted discussion outlining the solutions and benefit you can provide the customer.

5. The very best advice is to listen more than you talk.

6. Customers appreciate going out to dinner, or a ticket to a sporting event, but they value more, sales people and companies that can offer sound business advice and help.

7. When a customer says that your company is "their title company," you know you have reached an important emotional threshold.

8. What really gains the interest of the customer is to give them a good idea.

9. Sell like a consultant:
   - Look for how your title products and escrow services can be better aligned or integrated with the components of your customer's company.

   - Look for how the delivery of your title and escrow products can match up better with your customer's systems.

157

- Examine your own systems and business components to see what could be of benefit for your customer to use or adapt in some way.

10. Love what you do. Don't fear selling, love selling.

11. Ask for the order.

## DEVELOPMENT IDEAS\QUESTIONS FOR CHAPTER 9

1. Discuss with your sales staff how first contacts will be made with customer prospects and new customers.

2. Meet with your sales team to develop a set of questions for specific customers, you are targeting for increased business. Develop possible Status, Issue, Implication and Solution questions.

3. Review and evaluate the different ways your sales people are developing customer relationships. Identify ways sales staff can add consultative selling ideas to their sales tactics with specific customers.

4. Discuss in your sales meeting the difficulties each person has experienced in asking for the order.

# SALES CALLS
## CHAPTER 10

The fact that initial impressions are critically important would seem to guarantee that sales people would plan at least their first sales visits carefully. Yet in practice, this simple process is often overlooked both for initial and ongoing customer meetings. More often than not, sales staff report they know what they want to accomplish during their customer visits but do not take the time to write anything down or plan ahead of time.

In our experience, 'winging it' or spur of the moment thinking is not the best way to conduct a meeting. As management trainers, we write out ahead of time what we will say in our presentations. We often then take the additional step to practice what we will say in front of a mirror. Roger likes to practice his presentations in the car as he drives to see his customers. The same types of preparation apply to sales calls. Your time spent with the customer should be focused and efficient. The last thing you want in front of a customer is to look un-prepared or struggle to get your points across.

When we mention the word planning, most sales people voice concerns about losing time in the field. We are fond of saying if you measure it, people will do it. We need to come up with a catchy phrase to say that if you plan and prepare ahead of time, good results will follow.

Call plans or call reports are one way to prepare for a customer meeting. To effectively use a call plan, the first step is to ensure that any call plan is aligned with any larger company plan or strategy. If your company has a sales plan, then your call plans need to be aligned with your sales plan.

Territory plans, account plans, and call plans should follow from the overall sales plans. For example, the activities planned for a customer sales call should be aligned with the strategies and tactics that trace back to the sales plan. In developing a written sales call plan, we recommend six pieces of information necessary in your planning:

1. DATE
2. CUSTOMER & SITUATION
3. GOALS
4. COMPANY STORY / PITCH
5. CALL ACTIVITIES
6. FOLLOWUP

This information can be captured on a simple form or computer program. The purpose of this plan is to plan and track sales activities.

## EXAMPLE OF A SALES CALL PLAN

| | |
|---|---|
| Date | June 1, 2014. |
| Sales person | Roger Lubeck. |
| Activity | Lunch with Tom Harding. |
| Customer | Tom Harding is the biggest Realtor at C21 Geneva. |
| Situation | Currently we have no business from Tom. |
| Story | Word is Tom is unhappy with his closer. |
| Follow-up | Office visit with our closer Julie. |

Call plans focus on specific date(s) for a specific customer, limited sales behavior for a specific period of less than a week. Territory and account plans cover longer periods and focus on coverage, time management, and issues affecting a group of customers. Typically, a territory (area) or account plan will have these key elements:

1. PERIOD
2. SALES PEOPLE
3. CUSTOMER SEGEMENT
4. SALES PROJECTION
5. TACTICS and ACTIVITIES
6. ISSUES / BARRIERS
7. CALLS PLANNED   (TOTAL / PERIOD)
8. RESOURCES NEEDED

## EXAMPLE OF A SALES ACCOUNT PLAN

| | |
|---|---|
| Period | June, 2014. |
| Sales people | Roger Lubeck, Chris Hanson, Lynette Chandler. |
| Segment | C-21 in Geneva (25 Realtors). |
| Projection | 10 new orders. |
| Activities | Breakfast presentation with our closers at C21. |
| | Roger lunch with Tom Harding at C21 in Geneva. |
| | Chris lunch with Tina William at C21 in Geneva. |
| | Lynette lunch with Bill William at C21 in Geneva. |
| Situation | Currently we have business from two new Realtors. |
| | No business from the principles Tom, Tina, or Bill. |
| Story | Tom is unhappy with his closer. |
| Follow-up | Office visit by our closers Julie and Ed. |
| Contacts | 7 hours in 20 days. |
| Expense | $125.00 in meals/food. |

## EXPENSE TRACKING

Tracking the amount of resources you spend on each customer is an essential aspect of good sales management and business analysis. If you know what you spend on a customer, you can determine the return you receive on any investment. For example, if we spend $150.00 on food and gas to receive five new orders worth $3000.00 we can say that for every dollar spent we got

$20.00 back, or our sales expense is 5% of revenue. The key comparison to make for each customer is total revenue received versus ongoing expenses. In general, we recommend using a simple spreadsheet designed to track the following categories over time.

1.  Gross Revenue
2.  Orders
3.  Meals\Drinks
4.  Entertainment
5.  Gifts\promotions
6.  Sponsorships
7.  Marketing\resource materials
8.  Office expense for customer
9.  Travel\employee
10. Lodging\employee
11. Meals\employee
12. Other expenses
13. Expense Total

## CUSTOMER PROFILE

We like Customer Profiles because they provide a means for sales staff to interact and share information with the other employees in the company. The information in the profile also provides for a quick review prior to a sales call.

The information needed for the profile can be gathered and maintained by the sales person and then made available to the other staff that interacts with the customer. For example, closers can review the customer profile prior to a closing with the customer to gain insights on personal customer preferences. Production and processing staff should be aware of contact information and any special needs or requests the customer has made regarding service and communication preferences. Ideally, the profile will be in a program (database) that has fields for the following types of information:

Business Information

1. Customer name
2. Title
3. Company
4. Address
5. Key assistant's name
6. Key manager's name
7. Contact numbers and addresses including social media
8. Webpage addresses
9. Preference requirements
10. Order entry preferences
11. Status update\communication preferences
12. Commitment delivery preferences
13. Closing schedule preferences

14. Post-closing needs

15. Turn-time requirements

16. Web-services preferred


Personal Information

17. Nickname

18. Birthday\age

19. Spouse\partner name

20. Anniversary

21. Children

22. Home address

23. Hobbies\special interests

24. Favorite restaurants\sporting events\community events

25. Favorite charity

26. Board or organization membership

27. Survey or customer satisfaction ratings and dates

28. DiSC Personal Profile information

29. Profile type

30. DiSC behavioral tendencies to note

31. DiSC sales approach

32. Sales Calls / Contact Information

33. Date

34. Transaction\order number

35. Type of call

36. Activity

37. Notes for staff\feedback received

38. Results


Maintaining the profile database to keep the information current is important. The profile should be updated periodically. In developing a profile system, it is important to consider who has access to the profile, who can enter or modify information in the profile, and how the profile will be used.

## GUIDING PRINCIPLES FOR CHAPTER 10

1. If you plan and prepare ahead of time, good results will follow. Plan for results.

2. Call Plans, Account and Territory Plans submitted by sales staff should always be in alignment with the overall sales plans developed by a company.

3. Track the amount of resources you spend on a customer to help evaluate return on investment.

4. Electronic Customer Profiles provide an important tool for sales staff to prepare for customer visits and help aid production and escrow staff when they make customer contacts.

## DEVELOPMENT IDEAS\QUESTIONS FOR CHAPTER 10

1. Work with your sales staff to decide which types of planning documents and tools will help them prepare for their customer visits.

2. Discuss Call Reports, Expense Tracking and Customer Profile development for specific customers.

3. Discuss Account and Territory Plan development for different customer segments.

# CREATING A SALES PLAN
## CHAPTER 11

The purpose of this chapter is to help you create a simple sales/market plan. Rather than providing a highly structured format to follow, our intent is to present an outline that is not complicated and you can customize to meet your particular needs and planning structure. Our outline is not form driven. The format of your plan should be determined by you based on the information you have gathered and analyzed.

In our experience, owners want plans and managers and employees hate planning. This can be especially true with market or sales plans. All too often, a group will spend weeks or months developing a written plan only to have it sit in a file somewhere gathering dust until it is time to write the next year plan. The following are truths we have learned from owners and executives.

1. If the plan isn't written it isn't a plan.
2. Written plans are useless if not implemented.
3. Successful plans are managed.
4. Even the best plan will fail sometimes.

Having a written plan does not guarantee success and much of the real work with any plan is in implementation, management, and follow-through. Planning is a sign of business maturity. In good companies, planning is something done every year not just when times are bad. For many small businesses, written or expressed goals take the place of formal written plans. Owners who are competitive and goal driven will manage their operation around achieving specific goals. We simply use the market or sales plan as a way of writing goals and developing actions (tactics) to support those goals. Later in the chapter, we will discuss the challenge of implementing a plan. For now, we are going to start by examining the components of most market/sales plans.

In good business planning, having a budget and having a sales plan goes together. The sales plan is designed to drive revenue and work. The budget is designed to manage expenses and derive profit. Taken together, you have a simple business plan.

Because having a sales plan and a budget go together, there is something of the chicken and the egg problem. In our experience, the sales plan should be created first in a field-up process and then the budget is built top down based around the plan. Plans that are completely developed by executives may lack field experience and they lack employee buy-in. On the other hand, plans created by sales staff and managers may lack the stretch that an owner needs or expects. In our experience, the best plans are a combination of executive and sales staff working together. This work can be done in stages and by different people or groups.

The CBA sales plan includes the following sections:

- Executive Summary
- Market Analysis
- Customer Analysis
- Competitive Analysis
- Sales Forecast
- Goals and Objectives
- Strategies and Tactics

These sections are typically created by a team, but written by one person or a small group of writers. The first step in developing a sales plan is gathering company, customer, competitor, and market information. The second step is to analyze the information gathered. The third step is to write goals based on the data and analysis. The final step is to develop strategies and tactics (actions) designed to achieve the goals. In a combined sales plan and budget, there will be financial, sales, and operational goals along with the expense and profit. Sales plans and budgets drive the following:

1. Revenue goals
2. Operational goals
3. Cost of Sales
4. Labor Expense
5. Other Operational Expense
6. Profit

7. Profit Margin

We are going to discuss each of the sections of the sales plan in detail and describe the information you should have in each section.

## THE EXECUTIVE SUMMARY

The Executive Summary is the last section you write for your plan after you have completed all other sections. However, it is placed in the very front of the plan. The Executive Summary should be no longer than one page. When writing this summary, consider it may be the only section an executive reads.

The contents of the Executive Summary should include overview statements about the major revenue goals and financial performance measures of the company, the target markets and their size, the customer segments in the plan, and competitor threats or weaknesses that may lead to opportunities. In the final paragraphs of the summary, the major sales strategies and tactics you plan to implement should be outlined. Also at the end of the summary, any critical resources needed and contingency planning that will be required should be detailed.

In the three sections that follow the executive summary, the Market Analysis, Customer Analysis, and Competitive Analyses, we develop information that provides the foundation for the goals, objectives, strategies and tactics written later in the plan. Think of these analyses sections as the fuel that fires the engine.

# EXAMPLE OF AN
## EXECUTIVE SUMMARY

This year we plan to increase our gross revenue by 3% over last year. Our gross revenue goal is $3,545,000. We project that 45% of our revenue will come from the residential market. Commercial transactions will account for 15% of revenue. Lender transactions will account for 30 percent of our revenue while Attorney and Builder transactions will account for 6% and 4% of revenue respectively. Goals for open and paid order goals are 6,089 and 4,287 respectively.

Residential. Interest rates are projected to rise. If this happens, lender business is projected to decrease by 8 percent and we plan to counter this market trend by increased sales activity in the residential markets.

REO. New in the coming year, we will focus on REO business. Our plan is to create a special production team to facilitate and grow this business. We are projecting that five percent of our gross revenue will come from our REO segment.

North Region. We will open two new retail offices in the north regions of our state. These will give us statewide coverage. To support these offices, we will be hiring eight new staff, including two new sales associates.

Production Hub. We plan to finalize our centralized title production hub, which will service our escrow offices located throughout the state.

Improving our overall customer service continues to be a strategy. A new WOW customer service program will be implemented to improve our overall customer satisfaction ratings. Additional strategies include a new "First Order Program" for customer prospects and lost customers who place their first new orders with us. We will also be focusing on growing our FSBO segment and will be developing new sales tactics for this customer group, including the use of social networking and advertising on home buying search engines.

Our statewide sales strategies will include a continued emphasis on improving our technology capabilities. Sales associates will promote upgrades to our website, our on-line order processing systems, and the marketing of new mobile apps for Realtor agents.

One major threat that we plan to counter is the development of affiliated business arrangements by our top competitor in the southern region of the state. Sales associates will be working to strengthen our relationships in the area with key realtors and emphasizing our superior service capabilities and our in-house attorney expertise that our competitors do not have.

Security bank in the northern section of the state is rumored to be developing its own title production unit and we will be developing contingency plans for that market possibility.

MARKET ANALYSIS

The Market Analysis section consists of a description of your market geography and size, market demographics, your market position, relevant market trends and expected market growth. To describe your market geography, size, and demographics consider the following:

1. Market location
2. Market size in square miles
3. Major cities
4. Location of your office(s)
5. Current population of major cities, counties, regions
6. Changes in population
7. Current number of households
8. Change in households
9. New homes built
10. Average/median home prices
11. Average title premium and settlement fees
12. Homes sold in the past year
13. Title transactions or title revenue in past years

In your market analysis, summarize your company's overall position in terms of revenue, orders, and market share. Describe your market position in any of the business segments identified in your market description. You may want to provide a simple table or chart of market share, orders, closings, or revenue for past years to demonstrate trends. If possible, your performance should be compared to your competitors in some way. In some states, revenue and expense data are made available comparing title companies. Consider providing the following information for the last three years for both your company and the entire market.

MARKET INFORMATION

1. Residential Real Estate Revenue – resale
2. Residential Real Estate Revenue – new construction
3. Residential Real Estate Revenue – refinance
4. Commercial Real Estate Revenue
5. New construction permits
6. Title premium revenue
7. Escrow/settlement revenue
8. Refinances revenue
9. Residential closings
10. Commercial closings
11. Market growth projections

COMPANY INFORMATION

1. Title premium revenue
2. Escrow/settlement revenue
3. Other title related revenue (income)

4. Other income

5. Open orders

6. Paid orders

7. Closings

8. Your search/equity transactions (paid orders)

9. Your residential refinance transactions (paid orders)

10. Your sale/resale transactions (paid orders)

11. Your commercial transactions (paid orders)

12. Your market share in orders and revenue

To describe market trends, summarize any trends in your market or within specific segments likely to affect real estate sales, title customers, or title insurance in the next 12-24 months. Business practice trends should also be summarized. For example, consider the following:

- How is the real estate transaction accomplished in the market?

- Who controls the title order?

- Are there Affiliate Business Arrangements? How many and with whom?

- Is there legislation anticipated to affect the market?

- How is technology changing the market? How are your competitors using technology?

- What are the major industries in the market and will they have any effect on real estate?

To describe market growth, detail how the overall market and specific segments within the market are expected to grow, remain static or decline in the next year. For example, what is the revenue potential for the commercial, residential resale, lender, attorney, and, builder\developer business segments? Growth can be expressed in terms of real estate sales revenue, the number of potential customers or projected revenue. For example, what are Realtors, lenders, and developers projecting for their business in the next year? For each projection you list, you should indicate the source of the projection. Consider the following potential growth areas:

- Estimates of population change.
- Estimates of existing home sales.
- Estimates for new home sales.
- Estimates for search\equity transactions.
- Estimates for residential refinance transactions.
- Estimates for residential sale/resale transactions.
- Estimates for commercial transactions.
- Estimates for all additional business lines (e.g., REO).

The information you place in the Market Analysis section should pass these tests: Will this information help us in our overall planning? Does this information point out new important opportunities we should consider? Does this information point out potential threats that we will need to react to in some way? Does this information provide insights or ideas regarding possible sales strategies or tactics we should consider?

## THE CUSTOMER ANALYSIS

In this section, you are providing detailed information about the performance of the different customer groups you are serving or possibly will serve in the future. These groups include current customers, new customers and prospects, customer growth targets, and lost customers. Since these terms can be interpreted differently, here are the definitions we use:

- Current customers = customers that you are serving in the current year.
- New customers = customers that have placed an order with you in the current year.
- Prospects = potential future customers that you want to qualify.

- Customer growth targets = current customers who you will target for increased sales and for whom you will devote increased sales activity and resources.
- Lost customers = customers, you once served, then lost, but now you will qualify again.

To analyze your current customer base, we recommend sorting or segmenting your customers into different types of groups or categories. Segmentation will provide you with different ways to consider what types of sales strategies and tactics may be possible or most beneficial for the different customer types you have identified.

We recommend starting your segmentation by conducting an 80\20 Analysis of your current customer base using customer orders and revenue. As we indicated in Chapter Seven, performing an 80\20 analysis will help you identify which customers give you approximately 80 percent of your revenue and or approximately 80 percent of your orders.

Before you start your 80\20 analysis, a word of caution. The 80\20 principle is a rule of nature that seems to apply to business "generally." In one company, we found that 18% of their customers accounted for 79% of their revenue. Close enough! However, other times we have found the revenue to customer percentage was 80\10 or 80\40.

If your company does significant commercial work, you may want to separate that business in your analysis in the beginning creating an 80\20 analysis for commercial business and one for residential business. The reason: you may have commercial customers who only give you one or two commercial orders, but their associated revenue will place them high in your combined rankings. That is fine as long as you understand their ranking positions in relation to your customers who do exclusively residential business. The alternative is to complete one analysis for commercial and one for residential business.

To get started, create a spreadsheet or report where you list unique customer names in one column and then associate orders, closings, and revenue in the following columns. Next, take your YTD results on your spreadsheet and rank order the customers listed. Create two rankings, the first based on revenue and the second based on orders.

If you choose, you can create separate worksheets and rankings for additional segmentation categories. For example, for professional designations (Lender; Realtor; Builder, etc.), or transaction types (Refinance; Resale, etc.). You may also want to develop 80\20 analyses for individual offices or for the different regions or markets you serve.

Once your customers and their corresponding orders and revenue are ranked, you can determine the points or division lines in the rankings at which you have 80% of your orders and or revenue. If those division points closely follow the 80\20 principle, the customers above the division points, at the top of the rankings, will represent approximately 20% of the customers listed. To check this percentage, count the number of customers at and above your division point and divide that total by the total number of customers listed in your rankings. Multiply the resulting decimal by 100 to determine the percentage.

In examining your customer rankings, you may find you have more or less than 20% of your customers accounting for 80% of your revenue or orders. In essence, you are looking for the point in your rankings where the smallest number of customers are contributing the largest percent to your revenue or orders. We categorize the customers at and above this dividing point as your "A" customers. Your "A" customers not only give you the most revenue and orders, but they can be your most loyal customers.

The customers that fall below the "A" customer group can be segmented as your "B" and "C" customers. 'B" list customers are typically in the middle section of your rankings and represent customers, you have done business with but who have significant business they are giving to other companies. "C" list customers are typically in the lower third of your rankings and may represent customers with little future sales potential or customers new to the market.

Rather than trying to force fit your rankings to the 80\20 guidelines, many times when you look at a ranking list of customer names and numbers, you can see a natural break in order revenue or volume. That is, a natural break in the data, for example, the point at where you have customers who give you 10 orders or more a year, and the point at where you have customers who give you less than 10 orders per year. The important point to remember is that regardless of whether your rankings closely correspond to the 80\20 division guidelines we have discussed or not, the important function of your analysis is to determine which customers are your top performers and which customers should be considered in other ways for sales planning purposes.

Once you have sorted your current customers and the segments you have chosen by revenue and orders, you can dig deeper into examining the following factors for specific customers and customer groupings:

- Total number of transactions in the market.
- Total number of open orders.
- Total number of paid orders.
- Cancellation rates.
- Total revenue.
- Total revenue\orders by order or transaction type.

- Market share for each segment indicated by percentage of total revenue.
- Which customers are highly satisfied, neutral or dissatisfied?
- Which customers are new to your rankings from the previous year?
- Which customers listed in your rankings from previous years are now lost?
- Which customers or segments are trending upward or downward?
- Which customers or segments provide high order volume and high revenue versus those customers who provide lower volume with lower priced orders?

If you have expense information for your current customers, you can examine selected customers in your rankings for profitability. This part of your analysis can include actual sales expenses and estimates of work expense. Based on these data, you can analyze customers in the following categories:

- High revenue/high profit?
- High revenue/low profit
- Low revenue/high profit?
- Low revenue/low profit?

The first part of your customer analysis section should end with the identification of who among your current customers should be considered as key growth targets for sales for the New Year. Target customers are those select customers who will receive more sales time and expense. Your target customers should be discussed within the body of the customer analysis section and then listed in a separate table in the Goals and Objectives section of the plan. For each target, identify order and revenue objectives for the period of the plan. In listing customer targets, identify the customer segment they represent.

If you have customer growth targets for the current year and corresponding sales goals, an analysis of YTD results for these customers should be made. Your analysis should include these questions: For which targets have the goals been met? For which targets were goals not met and why? Consider presenting a table with YTD order and revenue results for these customers.

The second part of your customer analysis section should focus on customer prospects and the lost customers you are considering reengaging. If possible, provide a list or table of the current year total transactions in the market for these customers. Alternatively, you can list projections for current and future order and revenue totals. Where possible, identify the customer's preferred title company and the additional preferred real estate

185

vendors they are using. As a part of your analysis, identify the customer segment the customer represents.

Among your list of prospects and lost customers, identify customers who should be considered as key prospects or those that would have higher priority in terms of prospecting time and expense. Among your prospects and lost customers, consider the following:

1.  The total number of orders\revenue in the market for the current and previous year.
2.  Those customers who are highly loyal to another title company.
3.  Those customers who give less than 50% of their business to one title company.
4.  Those customers who are less than satisfied with their current vendors.
5.  Those customers with the highest potential.

Over time, you may gather additional information that is pertinent to the Customer Analysis section. For example, customer profile information or information gained from customer interviews. This ancillary information can be valuable in making decisions about sales strategies and tactics. Customer profile and interview information can be summarized in the appendix section of your plan.

## THE COMPETITIVE ANALYSIS

In this section, you are assessing your competitive strengths, weaknesses, and the opportunities or threats that exist within your markets. The analysis includes not only your own operations, but those of your competitors. Where a competitor is strong we call that aspect a threat. Where a competitor is weak we say we have an opportunity. Comparing your company's strengths and weaknesses against a competitor or the market in this way is called a SWOT (strengths, weaknesses, opportunities, threats) analysis. In a SWOT analysis, if you are strong and a competitor is weak, you have a potential advantage. Where you are weak and a competitor is strong, you face a potential threat and have a disadvantage.

One of the key characteristics of a SWOT analysis is, it should challenge or stimulate your thinking about possible sales strategy and tactics. The strengths you list should challenge you to think about opportunities. The weaknesses you list should challenge your thinking about threats in your markets and what counter measures may be necessary.

To organize your competitive information, first list your own strengths and weaknesses and then those of your top competitors. If you operate in different markets with different competitors, those should be considered separately. You may also want to detail strengths and weaknesses for specific customer segments.

The next step is to summarize the strengths and weaknesses you have identified and translate them to opportunities and threats. We recommend summarizing your SWOT analysis in a table like the example provided at the end of the chapter.

The starting point in your competitive analysis is your own operations. Provide a candid, fact-based assessment of your operational performance, service and customer issues. Begin with listing your strengths for your company as a whole. Next, detail specific strengths for particular customer segments or markets. Identify those features within your operations that add value to your product or to your customer's business. Evaluate your strengths by customer segment, for example, in terms of price, cost of production, marketing support, infrastructure, and technology. Strengths may relate to office locations, management talent, starter files, training, underwriting or the use of social networking. Strengths could also include human resources like people with knowledge in national business, underwriting, information systems and management. List any unique customer service that provides an advantage with a particular segment or customer group.

For weaknesses, consider service levels, customer needs that are unfulfilled, customer complaints, products or services for which a competitor has an advantage, and information you have gained from surveys or customer interviews.

After considering your own operations, analyze your competitor strengths and weaknesses. We have included an example competitor analysis at the end of this chapter.

Determining how many competitors to profile is a question. If you are number one in the market, your focus should be on the three to four competitors immediately below you. If your market share is lower, you should focus on who is going after your business and from which companies you can gain business.

The final step is to translate your competitive analysis into opportunities and threats. Opportunities and threats are typically of three types: those created by something you are doing or not doing; those created by something your competitors are doing or not doing; and those based on specific customer needs. Opportunities may be the result of market growth, business changes, serviceability, or the ability to offer greater value that will create a demand for your services.

Threats may include marketing or business practices, pricing, government regulation, new or anticipated competition, changes in the local economy, changes in consumer behavior, or changes in technology. Threats can also include factors beyond your control that could put your marketing or sales strategy, or the business itself, at risk.

189

The result of your SWOT analysis should be a synthesis of the critical issues that emerge from your strengths and opportunities balanced against your weaknesses and threats. The conclusions you draw in this section should provide a strong basis for the goals and objectives, strategies, and tactics you develop in the remaining sections of your plan.

## SALES FORECAST

The Sales Forecast is a summary section that is placed in the front of the plan, immediately following the Executive Summary. The Sales Forecast is completed after you have finished your market, customer, and competitor analyses. It is designed to provide a quick snapshot of your sales projections and revenues for the coming year. The Sales Forecast should provide greater detail about projected financial outcomes compared to what you have stated in the Executive Summary

Your sales forecast should be 1-4 paragraphs in length. The sales forecast should be clear and concise. In forecasting for the next year, you must take into consideration year-end projections and any projections for real estate nationally and in your area. Since sales planning typically takes place in the 4$^{th}$ quarter of the year before final year-end results are available, you have to have a sound basis for projecting annual revenue. In part, this will come from company statistics for the past three to five years, and any available data from the market.

## GOALS AND OBJECTIVES

This section includes overall revenue (financial) goals and objectives, customer segment goals and objectives, and objectives for current customer growth targets, prospects and lost customers.

People are always confused about the difference between goals and objectives. Objectives are simply smaller sub-steps or result increments we identify. They help us divide an outcome or result, we have indicated as a goal into smaller steps or parts. The key word here is outcomes. The goals and objectives, we write in this section must be measurable outcomes, not actions. The goals and objectives in this section do not explain "how" we will achieve the results we want or the process we will follow, just the outcomes we want to achieve. Begin by summarizing your overall revenue goals for the period of the plan. Include the following:

1. The total dollar revenue projected.
2. The average income per paid order, the goal is based on.
3. The number of open and paid orders to achieve goal.
4. The open/paid order ratio.

5.  The increase the revenue goal represents over the previous year.

Consider the following example of the opening sentences in the Goals and Objectives section:

"The overall revenue goal is $6,102, 360 and is based on an average of $847.55 per paid order. The open order goal is 9000. The paid order goal is 7,200 using a capture rate of 80%. The projected revenue goal represents a seven percent increase in revenue over the previous year."

Following the overall revenue goals for the company, describe the segment specific objectives that relate to achieving the overall company goals. For example:

> Forty-two percent of our revenue will be from the Realtor segment equaling 3024 paid orders. Thirty-eight percent of our revenue will come from the Lender segment, equaling 2736 paid orders. Fifteen percent of our revenue will come from the Attorney segment, equaling 1080 paid orders. The FSBO segment will represent 3.5 % of our revenue equaling 252 paid orders. One and a half percent of our total revenue will come from the builder\developer segment equaling 108 paid orders.

You can additionally consider indicating for each customer segment you include, the percentage increases or decreases your projections represent over the previous year. Tables or charts can be inserted into your plan to illustrate the different segment contributions to your overall revenue goal and the percentage increases or decreases your projections represent over previous years.

Deciding how detailed you should be in writing financial objectives for segments or sub-segments is a matter of functionality. In general, if you plan to have separate strategies and tactics for specific segments or sub-segments you should have corresponding objectives that speak to projected revenue and order outcomes.

For example, let us say that you have identified a group of 50 Realtor agents who now because of technology advances operate out of their homes instead of having an affiliation with a national Realtor company.

You decide that you want to market to this smaller group of agents and develop specific sales tactics expressly for this group. Because you will be taking different marketing steps with this group, and engaging in different tactics, there will be associated costs and resource allocations.

Having financial objectives for this Realtor sub-segment will help you analyze, after your plans have been implemented, whether your sales tactics are successful. Ultimately, the financial objectives you write will help you decide whether there was an adequate return on your investment.

The second half of the Goals and Objectives sections should be devoted to listing individual revenue and order objectives for customer growth targets (including new customers), prospects and lost customers. Each of these groups can be listed indicating the specific segments they represent and if applicable, showing the previous year's performance.

Tables can be used to organize these lists and will aid managers in readily tracking progress throughout a plan's implementation.

STRATEGIES AND TACTICS

In this final section of your plan, describe the sales strategies and tactics you will use to achieve the financial goals and objectives you have developed. Strategies are the overarching concepts that describe how you will reach a goal. Tactics are the specific actions you will perform to implement the strategy.

To illustrate the difference between strategy and tactics, let us say your overall revenue goal represents an increase of seven percent over the previous year and within the Realtor segment alone you are planning an increase of 10 percent. One of the strategies for your Realtor segment will be to increase sales coverage throughout your region. Your sales tactics for this strategy will be to hire two new sales people; account managers will commit to calling on customer growth targets within the segment once per week and to visit all remaining "A" and "B" customers within the segment once per month. Remember, goals and objectives represent outcomes; strategies and tactics represent how you will achieve the outcomes you are trying to achieve.

The strategies and tactics you develop should flow logically from the analysis sections of your plan and the goals and objectives you have set. Typically, strategies and tactics are developed for implementation company-wide, followed by those set for specific segments, regions or individual offices.

In our many years of consulting, we have seen title companies develop strategies and corresponding sales tactics in the following areas:

- Alliances
- Consumer marketing
- Customer focus
- Education and training
- Location and convenience
- Marketing support
- Product value
- Regional versus national business
- Relationship development
- Sales coverage
- Service excellence
- Service features
- Social networking

- Technology
- Website development

The strategies and tactics you choose for your plan should be based on a thorough analysis of what was successful from the current and previous years. This means identifying the strategies and tactics that produced favorable results and those that did not and why? Reviewing the tactics that were successful with individual customer targets is also important in deciding what will be relied on again.

A final consideration in this last section of your plan is to develop sales tactics for individual customer growth targets, prospects or lost customers for whom you want to direct special attention or resources. List the customers and then detail the specific sales tactics you will follow for each customer in question. The following is an example of a company-wide strategy and the corresponding tactics:

Strategy: Promote the new technology projects of the company.

Tactic 1: Market online, web-based ordering procedures.

Tactic 2: Schedule training with customers for new features on company website.

Tactic 3: Promote use of mobile closing team.

Tactic 4: Use social media to promote company, services and products.

Tactic 5: Promote and demonstrate downloading and use of special Apps from web site.

The following is an example of a segment specific strategy and the corresponding tactics:

Strategy: Develop new customer sources in the Lender Segment.

Tactic: Expand focus to private banking institutions.

Tactic: Call on local Credit Unions.

Tactic: Identify potential new lender partners within state.

Tactic: Identify potential national business lender partners

Tactic: Attend 1-3 national lender conferences.

## IMPLEMENTATION STEPS

We said in the beginning of this chapter it is not uncommon for sales plans to be developed and then sit idle and not used throughout the year. Of course, this is not what you want. The sales plan should be used as a road map to not only direct sales activity monthly but also as a tool to monitor and track progress and foster accountability among sales staff and managers as well as all the employees of the company. For years, we have worked with sales managers who monthly sit down with their account managers to review progress with their customer targets. These sales

197

managers often turn straight to the Goals and Objectives section of the sales plan to review the order and revenue projections made, discuss YTD progress and then review what strategies and tactics are working, which are not and why.

The planning process takes time. We recommend developing a yearly planning cycle that starts in September of each year. Here are our recommended timelines:

September:

Convene a planning team to start the planning process. The team should consist of sales staff, managers, and key decision makers, but also should include representation from the other functional areas of the company. We think having a closer or processor sit in with this team is a great idea. The first task of this team is to review the major components of the sales plan and make work assignments.

October:

The sales planning team convenes to review progress on assignments and discuss preliminary findings and ideas. Market and company data should be coming in.

November:

First written drafts for all major assignments for the plan are due. The team convenes to review progress and discuss needed additions or changes in the planning process. Third quarter YTD order counts and revenue numbers are reviewed. Also discussed is a YTD 80\20 analysis of customer rankings. YTD progress for customer growth targets and new customers is also reviewed. End of fiscal year order count and revenue projections should also be discussed. By mid-November, feedback is given back to team members on assignment drafts. The lead sales manager is typically responsible for the feedback.

December:

Final drafts for all major sections of the sales plan are due for executive review and feedback. By late December, 4th quarter numbers and year-end projections are added to the plan and final feedback is given to team members for section assignments.

1st Quarter:

Implement the plan. At the start of the New Year, review the entire sales plan with account managers, sales managers and production staff. Focus especially on the sales strategies and tactics.

2nd Quarter:

At the end of the first quarter, review the plan goals and objectives, sales strategies and tactics, with all sales managers and Account Representatives. Discuss whether timelines are being met for the actions planned and make any adjustments needed based on progress. Review each month, YTD results for growth targets.

3rd Quarter:

At the end of the 2nd quarter, make needed adjustments to sales strategies and tactics that are not producing needed results. Consider any budget and operation changes before the end of the third quarter. Check customer-service satisfaction levels for all "A" customers to ensure that high levels of service are being maintained for your top customers. Check progress on all financial goals and objectives. Make adjustments in coverage and resource allocations.

4<sup>th</sup> Quarter:

Track results related to the plan and make adjustments. At the beginning of the 4<sup>th</sup> quarter, start preparing for the development of the new sales plan for the coming year.

CUSTOMER ORDER AND REVENUE OBJECTIVES TABLE

| CUSTOMER | TYPE | SEGMENT | ORDERS | REVENUE |
|----------|------|---------|--------|---------|
| Amy Abbott | Growth Target | Realtor | 25 from 18 | $21,188 |
| George Jenkins | Growth Target | Lender | 15 from 10 | $12,731 |
| Jerry Lugent | Prospect | Builder | 5 | $4,237 |
| Alice Watson | Prospect | Attorney | 8 | $6,780 |
| Judy Wilson | Lost Customer | Realtor | 10 | $8,475 |

## COMPETITOR ANALYSIS EXAMPLE

| COMPETITOR | STRENGTHS | WEAKNESSES |
|---|---|---|
| Acme Title | • Number #1 in market share<br>• Convenient locations<br>• Professional looking closing offices<br>• Long History in community<br>• Experienced and aggressive sales staff | • Slow turn-time<br>• Behind on technology<br>• Recent customer service issues |
| For Certain Abstract | • Strong ties with attorney segment<br>• Reputation for handling difficult files<br>• Highly experienced examiners<br>• Staff have long tenure with company<br>• Reputation for doing quality work | • Not attracting younger clientele<br>• Behind on technology<br>• Leadership slow to change<br>• Employee complaints about leadership |
| Easy Answers Title | • Young, energetic staff, including leadership<br>• Uses latest technology<br>• Attracting new Realtors<br>• Weekend closings<br>• Mobile closings<br>• Strong interactive website<br>• Use of social networking | • High staff turnover rate<br>• Complaints from established customers<br>• Technology applications are not well integrated<br>• Inexperienced sales staff. |

## SWOT ANALYSIS EXAMPLE

| STRENGTHS | WEAKNESSES |
|---|---|
| • Multiple closing offices in good locations<br>• Large footprint across the Region<br>• Weekend closings<br>• In-house attorneys<br>• Mobile applications on website<br>• Specific marketing for FSBO segment<br>• Expertise in short sales and REO. | • Lack of centralized production<br>• Slow turn-time<br>• In-experienced sales staff<br>• New employee orientation<br>• Poor management structure<br>• Management training<br>• Lack of experience in builder-developer segment |
| OPPORTUNITIES | THREATS |
| • Main competitor closing office<br>• Ability to attract national business<br>• Technology interface with Realtors<br>• Increased use of technology for social networking | • Labor ratios are too high<br>• Key competitors gaining ground with processing technology<br>• Loss of key sales staff<br>• Customer service levels<br>• Lack of leadership in some offices causing morale problems |

## GUIDING PRINCIPLES FOR CHAPTER 11

1. Even the smallest title agency can be more successful with a formal written sales plan.

2. Develop a yearly planning cycle for sales plans. Start in September of each year and combine a "field up" and "top down" approach to gathering information and formulating ideas.

3. The Market, Customer and Competitor Analyses sections of the sales plan help fuel our thinking about what directions our sales efforts should take in the coming year.

4. To analyze your current customer base, sort or segment your customers into different types of groups or categories. Segmentation will aid in identifying different strategies and tactics for the different types of customers you serve.

5. Consider creating an 80\20 analysis for commercial business and one for residential business.

6. Your "A" customers contribute the largest percent of your revenue or orders and are likely your most loyal, important, and consistent customers. Look at your "B" and "C" customer groupings from your 80\20 analyses to identify customers for increased sales opportunities.

7. In a SWOT analysis, if you are strong and a competitor is weak you have a potential advantage. Where you are weak and a competitor is strong, you face a potential threat and have a disadvantage.

8. Objectives are simply smaller sub-steps or result increments that we identify for the goals we develop. The goals and objectives, we write must be measurable outcomes, not actions. Goals and objectives do not explain "how" we will achieve the

results we want or the process we will follow, just the outcomes we want to achieve.

9.  Sales Strategies and Tactics explain "how" we will achieve our goals and objectives.

10. Strategies are the overarching concepts that describe how you will reach a goal. Tactics are the specific actions you will perform to implement the strategy.

## DEVELOPMENT IDEAS\QUESTIONS FOR CHAPTER 11

1.  Commit to a formal sales planning process for your company. Identify a team of employees, managers and or sales staff to help develop your sales plan.

2.  Review the components of the sales plan outlined in this chapter and identify members of the team to work on the different sections. Set development timelines and have the team meet regularly to review plan drafts and discuss refinements.

3.  Start the planning process in the fall of the year so that you will be ready to start with plan implementation at the first of the New Year.

4.  Review and evaluate your sales plan results with the team, at least quarterly, as you progress through the year. Make needed adjustments to the sales plan when needed.

# MANAGING SALES

## CHAPTER 12

Several years ago, Chris was asked to facilitate a sales meeting for a national underwriter. The goal of the meeting was to review the sales plan for the coming year including new sales strategies and tactics. At the meeting, Chris was surprised by the small turnout given the large number of sales people working in the region. When Chris asked the sales manager about the attendance, the manager said he had problems getting the sales staff to attend meetings. He explained he made attendance at meetings optional, especially if the salesperson had more important things to do.

The premise of this chapter is the effectiveness and success of a sales force is determined by its management. Selling may be an art. Some say sales people either have a talent for selling or they do not. We believe sales skills can be taught. However, sales management is not an art. A good sales manager is a person who has learned a set of skills. An effective sales manager is someone who understands selling and understands motivating and managing salespeople. Typically, the best sales person does not make a good sales manager. In our experience, a top seller is often a highly competitive loner who is motivated solely by personal gain. To be an effective sales manager you need to be a team player, competitive, but focused on the organization. A good sales manager is organized and a good planner. A sales manager needs to create and follow a sales plan, hold structured meetings with staff, track progress using metrics, and, keep people motivated and yet accountable. An effective sales manager sets clear expectations, establishes sales objectives, links sales activities and tactics to goals and objectives, and manages people accordingly.

In this chapter, we focus on the components of the sales management process. These components include: sales planning, setting goals and expectations, using performance measures, account management, monitoring and directing sales activity, time management, and conducting good sales meetings.

Debbie Collins is a Vice President and Director of Sales at Meridian Title Corporation in Indiana. Debbie and her sales managers use sales plans as a key component throughout the year to work with the Meridian sales staff. Here is what Debbie has to say about sales management and sales planning.

> Creating a formal sales plan was the single best strategy we implemented to create a true sales focus for our account managers, sales managers and, ultimately, our company. Our sales managers are thorough in their research of market trends, as well as competitive and customer analysis. Our account managers become participants in the success of their markets by creating targets and strategies to help reach our revenue goals. Writing these annual sales plans also creates cohesive goals for all our managers, and even employees, as they are shared throughout the company. We definitely see our success measured and achieved through our sales planning process.

THE SALES PLAN

For over thirty years, Ken Lingenfelter worked in the title industry. Starting in high school and working while in college, Ken went from owning one Metropolitan Title office with two employees in 1978 to a company with over fourteen hundred employees, offices in fourteen states, and a sales force as good as any in the business when he sold the company in 2003.

CBA started working with Ken in 1994. Our focus was on designing and implementing processes to help Ken and his executives lead and manage a growing company. In that time, we developed for Metropolitan Title and others a Sales Planning Process that they used throughout the year. When asked why he made his office managers and sales staff develop a written sales plan, Ken said, "A plan isn't a plan unless it's written!"

Even today as President of Lingenfelter Performance Engineers, Metropolitan Motor Sports, and The Lingenfelter Collection, Ken is a firm believer in having an annual written sales and business plan with a budget.

Having an annual sales plan and sales goals is essential to a business. Once a plan is established, creating accountability with the plan is critical to making the plan come alive. Too often, a plan is written and then sales staff goes back to doing what they have always done. Creating a link between the written sales plan and the week-to-week management of the individual account representatives (sales staff) is a basic component of sales management. The sales plan essentially provides a road map for sales activities (action) and expected outcomes from those activities (results). The sales plan helps to translate the company's financial goals into sales strategy and tactics, actions to be used with customers. In our experience, there are five levels of planning.

1. Strategic plans
2. Business plans
3. Sales goals and sales plans
4. Customer goals and account plans
5. Call plans

Strategic plans develop financial and operational goals, strategies, and tactics for a company over a period more than a year.

Business plans and budgets, develop financial and operational goals, objectives, and tactics for a company over a period of a year.

Sales plans translate the financial goals and strategies the company has identified, often in its business plan or budget, into goals and actions for specific customer segments and markets.

Account plans are developed by the individual sales person for customer targets, prospects, and their assigned accounts.

Call plans are developed by sales staff for specific customers, for a given time period, and detail when calls and other customer activities will take place and what they will consist of.

Each account representative should be able to turn to the sales plan and see the specific outcomes that are expected and the sales tactics and activities expected within specific customer segments. It is up to the Sales Manager working with the account representative to help the translation from the sales plan to the actions taking place for specific customers.

In the 2003 film comedy, *Lost in Translation*, Bill Murray plays an American actor, Bob Harris, who has been sent to Japan to shoot a commercial endorsing a whiskey brand called "Santori." The problem is that Bob does not speak the language. When the Japanese director calls out directions on the set to Bob, something gets lost in translation, and both the director and Bob become frustrated. What is written in a sales plan should not seem like a foreign language. The sales manager is the director. His/her communication is the key to helping the sales people translate the plan into action. Here is an example of the translation from the sales plan to specific activity on the part of the account representative:

## SALES PLAN TO CALL PLAN

| | |
|---|---|
| Segment: | Realtors |
| Goal: | To increase overall gross revenue for the segment by ten percent over previous year levels, by the end of the fiscal year. |
| Strategy: | Increase focus on new Realtors. |
| Objective: | To increase orders by 40 percent from Realtors new to the market, over previous year levels, by the end of the fiscal year. |
| Tactic: | Provide training to new Realtors. |
| Tactic: | Provide special operations handling for first orders placed by new Realtors. |
| Account Plan: | Identify and target 25 new Realtors in southern region of company who match the profile of the Companies' "A" customers. |
| Call Plan: | Call on five new Realtor targets per month. Introduce company, provide elevator speech, enroll in training classes for new Realtors; explain special handling procedures for new orders placed. |

## SETTING EXPECTATIONS

As Business Psychologists, we are often asked by managers to help with improving an individual's performance. As simple as it seems, the first step in managing sales performance is telling sales people what is expected of them. Often this step is neglected or the expectations discussed are not clear to the sales person. A simple test for any sales manager is asking the sales person directly,

> "Tell me what is expected of you each week and at the end of each month?"

If staff are unclear what is expected of them, provide the employees with a written statement of expectations. Beyond that, you might provide examples and non-examples of behavior that demonstrates implementing what is expected. For example, if <u>being a leader in providing technology</u> is a part of your overall company vision, you can provide specific examples of how that aspect of the vision can be carried out. For example, discuss and demonstrate how the company's new phone App allows customers to place orders.

For new sales staff, understanding what is expected in terms of the company's overall culture and the direction that has been set is especially important. Providing a comprehensive orientation in the first days of employment will help make expectations clear from the start.

For additional information on setting expectations, we recommend referring to our first book, *Finding the Right Path: A Guide to Leading and Managing A Title Insurance Company*[27]. In Chapter 10, we discuss the basic ideas that should be considered in working with all employees to set clear expectations.

In 1954 Peter Drucker, in his book *The Practice of Management*, coined the term "management by objectives" to refer to the process of defining objectives to specify what is expected of employees. In talking to managers over the years, we know there is frequent confusion over the difference between goals and objectives. Here are two simple rules to follow when writing goals and objectives:

Goals and objectives clearly define measurable outcomes or results we want to accomplish in the future.

Objectives are a sub-set of a goal or the intermediate increments toward the results you are seeking.

In theory, if all the objectives are met, the goal is achieved. From our previous sales plan example, here are a goal, an objective, and a sales tactic that defines for the sales person what is expected:

---

[27] Roger Lubeck and Chris Hanson, *Finding The Right Path: A Guide To Leading and Managing A Title Insurance* Company (Sugar Grove, Illinois: iiWii Press, 2011).

Goal example (outcome): For the accounts you work on, we expect a 10 percent increase in revenue from the Realtor segment, over the previous year's level, by the end of the fiscal year.

Objective example (outcome): For the accounts that you work on, we expect a 40 percent increase in orders from Realtors new to the market, over the previous year's levels, by the end of the fiscal year."

Tactic example (process): Start providing training to new Realtors in the market by the end of the first quarter."

Ultimately, the goals and objectives you write should not only specify what is expected, but there should be a clear path connecting them to the overall goals, strategies and tactics written in the sales plan.

One of the initial ideas of management by objectives was to engage the employee in jointly discussing and ultimately writing down what is expected. For the Sales Manager, formally writing down the goals and objectives established with Sales Staff, and reviewing progress frequently, are essential steps for good management. We also love the idea of conducting sessions with sales staffs in which they initially help provide input regarding the goals and objectives established. The greater amount of input you

213

can gain from staff in this process, the greater ownership, there will be on the part of the sales staff to invest and successfully carry out the planned actions.

There are several reasons Sales Managers fail in setting clear and specific expectations. Avoid these traps and you will be on your way to better sales management. First, document your expectations and make sure the sales person has a copy. Since the goals and objectives you write will be measured, you will want to refer to them often and discuss them in your individual meetings with staff. We encourage Sales Managers to use hard copy in meetings with sales staff. Walking into a meeting with hard copy and reviewing each goal and objective one by one sends a strong message the performance expectations set are important.

Your meetings to review goals, objectives, sales strategies and tactics should be formal, sit-down affairs. You cannot casually stand over someone's cubicle and carry out a successful performance review discussion. Most importantly, setting expectations without frequent and consistent monitoring and feedback on the part of the sales manager is short sighted. You should monitor sales performance monthly and provide feedback. If feedback and especially acknowledgement and praise for work well done are not delivered by the sales manager on a timely basis, the chances are greater it will not be as effective. The more timely the better. Monthly will be effective, but weekly will be even better.

If you see that a sales person has just landed a first order from a new customer, seek that sales person out and praise the performance as soon as you can.

## USING PERFORMANCE MEASURES

We have stressed for many years in our consulting the old adage, if you measure it, people do it. We first saw a demonstration of this simple idea back in our early training as researchers. Chris was asked to observe several teachers in their classrooms to determine the amount of praise they were providing to their students. He first just sat and observed in each classroom, but did not tell the teachers what he was looking at. In actuality, he was counting the number of praise statements teachers made to their students. As a second step in the research, the teachers were told exactly what Chris was observing and recording. To no one's surprise, the praise rates of the teachers increased significantly. The concept has been duplicated in many different fields and it is true for sales behavior. Sales Managers cannot spend all their time observing what sales people do, but they can measure specific sales results and activities and hold salespeople accountable. Using measurable results, the Sales Manager can reward and praise each sales person when he/she achieves or exceeds a goal.

In addition to translating performance expectations directly from the company sales plan, there are a number of performance measures sales managers can consider to set expectations and also track and monitor performance and sales activities. Our advice is to select a smaller number of performance measures to start with. The last thing you want is to have heads spinning because your sales people are accountable to an overly long list of metrics. Focus first on a few measures that meet your needs from the two lists below. As you become proficient at using these measures, as your sales people see their benefit, and as your results dictate, add additional metrics to your tool bag to increase the sophistication of your approach.

The following is a listing of performance measures to use to establish goals and outcome objectives and track results. Each of these can be written for specific time periods (e.g., monthly, quarterly, by year's end).

1. Total Revenue
2. Total Expenses
3. Revenue and orders from existing customers
4. Revenue and orders from new customers
5. Revenue and orders from target customers
6. Revenue and orders from customers in specific customer groups (segments)
7. Revenue and orders from lost customers
8. Revenue per segment

9. Number of new customers

10. Customer satisfaction ratings

The tracking of outcome results should not be the sole strategy a sales manager uses to manage the Sales Team. The monitoring and management of sales activity is also important and ideally there should be a good mix of both outcome metrics and process metrics. The following are a list of process metrics that can be used for different time periods:

1. Sales calls per week

2. Sales calls per week per customer type

3. The number of new customers or prospects to identify

4. Completing account plans

5. Completing sales journals

6. Percentage of time spent on new customers

7. Percentage of time spent on prospects

8. Percentage of time spent on existing customers

9. Percentage of time spent on inactive customers

10. Percentage of time spent on lost customers

## MONITORING AND DIRECTING SALES ACTIVITY

For Sales Managers it is important to track and monitor results and set expectations based on results. Unfortunately, Sales

Managers tend to be better at telling sales people what they want as opposed to helping them get results.

The key for a sales manager is to work with the salesperson to not only review results periodically but also discuss what sales activities and tactics are working or not working. We advocate taking the process one-step further. Sales managers need to be working with their sales staff to help identify sales strategies and tactics based on the results. What we are advocating is for sales managers to engage in a more interactive, dynamic process with their sales staff. The sales manager can first make sure the salesperson is following what is outlined in the sales plan. Next, the sales manager can monitor sales results and activities using the performance measures developed. The manager in turn can provide feedback based on results but also work with the salesperson to modify sales strategies and tactics for specific customers or customer segments when needed.

In part, what the sales manager can facilitate is critical thinking on the part of the sales person. For example, in planning for the sales call, the sales manager can review with the sales person:

1. The objectives of the sales call.
2. What is known about the customer's needs and values.
3. What questions to ask the customer.
4. The customer's sales history.

5. What sales tactics have been successful and which have not.

6. What the competition is offering.

7. What objections might arise.

8. What types of follow-through should be discussed.

After the sales call the sales manager can debrief the results of the call with the sales person. When called for, this type of review can include the follow-through and logistics needed when the customer places an order.

When managers sit down with their sales people in individual meetings, a set agenda is important. A set agenda can consist of reviewing goals, objectives and plans, comparing plans to YTD results and reviewing sales strategies and tactics. Coaching and problem solving should also be standard tools in the Sales Managers toolbox. Sales Managers will find themselves in trouble when they focus too heavily on numbers instead of a plan, do not focus on necessary sales actions, and do not set priorities.

We have heard for many years from Sales Managers that sales people hate to take the time to submit call plans and call journals. Our answer has always been to use a functional approach: let the results determine what steps you need to take to direct your sales staff. If sales staff are meeting their goals and objectives, insisting on highly regimented call plans and call reports may not be warranted. In fact, they may as sales people will say, get in the way. However, if results are not what are expected, then more highly defined call plans and the use of journals are warranted as a way to monitor, review, and direct sales activity. In today's electronic portable on-line environments, the process of recording and monitoring sales activity has become much more efficient and user friendly.

One final note on call plans and journals. We do not want to dismiss the importance of consistent communications between the sales manager and sales staff nor with operations. Good and frequent communications about actions and logistics with customers are paramount. Absent the use of communication means like e-mail, phone discussions, face-to-face interactions, or notes in computer fields, call plans and journals can provide a valuable communication function. One area where sales managers can take a more proactive approach is time management.

TIME MANAGEMENT

For the sales person the question often is "How can I allocate my time for the customers I have been assigned?" Here is a time management activity the sales manager can use with their sales staff. In a meeting, or individually, have the salesperson complete the following table. They should complete the second column to the right writing in the percentage of time they believe they should be spending in a month's time with the customer types listed in the column to the left. When completed the percentages should add up to 100 percent.

| Customer Type | % of Time Spent |
|---|---|
| Target Growth Accounts | |
| Customer Prospects | |
| New Customers | |
| Existing "A" Customers | |
| Existing "B" and "C" Customers | |

You can have the sales person complete the table and discuss whether you agree with the time percentages or whether you would like to see some adjustments. If the sales person serves multiple markets or territories, you can have them complete a table for each region they serve.

Of course, once there is agreement on how time will be allocated, the real test is to compare actual time usage one month later with the sales person. Again, we prefer a functional approach to using this type of monitoring. If the sales person is meeting their sales goals and objectives, time management may not be an issue. On the other hand, if improvement is called for, the sales manager can monitor and direct time management through the use of call reports and journals of some type.

The review of call reports and journals on the part of the sales manager often leads to the discussion of call patterns. For example, if the manager knows the sales person has allocated 30 percent of their time to target growth accounts, the next question can be the frequency at which these customers are called upon within a specific period. In reviewing call patterns, sales managers can check and discuss with sales staff, customer geographic locations to ensure the best and most efficient use of travel time.

## MEETINGS WITH YOUR SALES TEAM

If you have more than one sales person, regular team meetings is a good idea and we highly encourage the use of team meetings. We know of no better place for sales people to get new sales ideas and tactics than from other sales people. The value of any team meeting is the synergy that can take place among team members sharing information and brainstorming.

As you probably know by now, we like meetings with set agenda and sales meetings are no exceptions. We like to see the sales meeting agenda include:

1. A review of overall company results: monthly paid order counts, revenue and capture rates.

2. A review of results by customer groups or segments (e.g., target growth accounts; "A" customers; new customers; prospects, etc.). Each sales person can present and discuss their individual account results.

3. A review of progress on the company sales plan. Review goals and objectives and compare actual results to what the plan sets forth. Also review the major strategies and tactics in the plan.

4. A discussion of which strategies and tactics are getting good results, which are not, and why.

5. A discussion of new sales opportunities or customer prospects.

6. Brainstorming on new ideas.

7. Customer satisfaction results and discussion.

8. Industry news and what is happening\trending in the market place.

9. The changes in plans that are in order and what specific new actions will take place.

10. A review of timelines, summary of decisions made, next team meeting date.

Through the years, we have discovered a number of meeting ideas that have been successful working with various sales teams. You can incorporate these ideas into your agenda as time permits or use one or two to add interest or something new. Here are ten tips:

1.  Devote a portion of the meeting to selling techniques.
2.  Critique a competitor's strengths and weaknesses.
3.  Role-play a customer meeting, sales call, or customer interview.
4.  Have a brainstorming session over a problem or issue.
5.  Ask a department or another team within your company to present what they do.
6.  Ask a customer to come and present information about the customer's business.
7.  Hold a meeting at a customer's office.
8.  Rotate meeting facilitation responsibility among sales people.
9.  Recognize outstanding performance at the end of the meeting.
10. Have staff at the end evaluate the meeting.

## GUIDING PRINCIPLES FOR CHAPTER 12

1. The effectiveness and success of a sales force is determined by its management.

2. A good sales manager is organized and a good planner.

3. The Sales Manager, working regularly with the sales staff, helps translate the sales plan to the actions taking place for specific customers.

4. The first step in managing sales performance is telling sales people what is expected of them.

5. The greater amount of input you can gain from sales staff in setting expectations, goals and objectives, the greater ownership, there will be on the part of staff to invest and successfully carry out the planned actions.

6. If feedback and praise for work well done are not delivered by the sales manager on a timely basis, the chances are it will not be effective. The more timely, the better.

7. If you measure it, (and sales people know you are measuring it) sales behavior will improve.

8. Let results determine what steps you need to take to direct your sales staff.

9. Regular sales team meetings are a good idea and we highly encourage their use. Their value is the synergy that can take place among team members sharing information and brainstorming.

## DEVELOPMENT IDEAS\QUESTIONS FOR CHAPTER 12

1. Take an inventory of your sales management practices. Answer these questions:

   a. Have clear expectations been communicated to your sales staff? Are these expectations in writing?

   b. Does the behavior of your sales staff match what has been planned in your sales plan?

   c. Do you ask for frequent input and ideas from your sales staff?

   d. Do you provide frequent feedback and praise to your sales staff for their work?

   e. Are the metrics you use to monitor and track sales behavior, adequate to provide good management and oversight?

   f. Are the reporting systems, you have in place adequate to communicate sales staff behavior?

   g. Do you have regular sales team meetings?

# SALES IN THE DIGITAL AGE
## CHAPTER 13

The Digital Age, Information Age, or Computer Age began in the 1970s and was defined as a period in which the goal was to have a computer in every office or home in America. Given the number of computers in existence in America by the 1990s, we have met the goal at least numerically, and effectively in the 2000s, we have moved into the next age, the Age of the Internet. In this chapter, we focus on the changing landscape of sales in the Age of the Internet.

In the last ten years, the internet has dramatically changed the culture and the way business is done. Today, customers can order title work using a digital App on smart phones or tablets. Very soon, internet glasses will be used to read and work on a virtual web. Without question, the new consumer has moved beyond the desktop or laptop computer. The question is where is the title industry?

All of the title companies we work with use the internet for e-mail and have a web site of some sort. The problem is the operating systems and production processes being used today were designed in the early days of the Computer Age. They are using a patchwork of software systems from the 2000s.

The existence of the internet created the opportunity for social media and social networking. Many futurists believe the boom of social networking defines a new era. It is changing the way people interact and changing the way companies and individuals sell.

In the 1990's we had a number of meetings with executives at Chicago Title to discuss how the title underwriters and agents could gain a position in the front of the real estate transaction channel. At that time, in many residential markets, Realtors had the most influence over the order and as such were in the front of the channel. Then, as now, Realtors, lenders, and attorneys all have more control over the placement of a title order.

One strategy being used to get to the front of the channel was entering into affiliated business arrangements. For example, there were title companies that owned a Real Estate Company. From the consumer's perspective, having the title work completed by the Realtor or lender meant one less stop. Thus, the idea of one-stop shopping was introduced.

Fast-forward twenty years and the same concept, getting to the front of the real estate transaction channel is still a relevant and important strategy for sales. However, a new player is fighting for a position at the head of the channel, the consumer.

Today sellers and buyers begin with the internet. They interact and learn about real estate companies over the internet, and may make their first or only contact over the web.

Companies like Zillow are creating a significant change in the ways consumers interact with real estate. New title applications are changing the way products are ordered and purchased. The title industry historically has been slow to change and adapt and it is likely to continue that way. Nonetheless, significant change is coming and cannot be stopped.

The internet provides an easy way for customers to research, study, explore, compare, and reach decisions entirely on their own. The advantage of the internet is there are no advisors, no gatekeepers, filters, or go-betweens. If a customer wants to find the best title company in Pittsburg or the best closer in Beaumont, Texas, all he has to do is type a line into a search engine, or ask Siri. In the past, the customer would have to ask or rely on their Realtor or Attorney.

Now, instead of asking a Realtor, the new buyer or seller goes to Zillow and before he/she asks an attorney, he/she asks Legal Zoom. The tendency to go to the internet and use the internet to find an attorney, lender, Realtor, or title company has implications for the real estate industry for years to come. The fact that customers are sharing what they experience with a company over the internet is just as important as the evolving freedom and power of the internet.

From now on, when a buyer has a bad closing they will tweet or text peers, associates, friends, and in some cases, anyone who cares to listen. Electronic platforms like Facebook, Twitter, Google +, LinkedIn, Instagram, YouTube, Pinterest, Klout, Foursquare, and Quora are examples of networks customers are using to engage with others when they pick up their smart phones, tablets and other mobile devices.

It is easy to be swept up in the enthusiasm over social networks and the new emerging digital technologies. In reality, the standard profile for a successful Realtor is still a middle-aged female who got her start in real estate long before she was making daily posts on her Facebook page. Nonetheless, by 2025, seventy-five percent of the workforce will be made up of Millennials, those born between the early 1980's and the early 2000's.

Last year a friend of Chris's was standing in line waiting for a presentation at the now famous South by Southwest Music Festival in Austin, Texas. He commented that most of the people in their 20's standing in line were engaged with their electronic devices and that behavior continued when they sat down inside and all the way through the presentation. Ironically, the topic of the presentation was the new social connectivity.

Chris's friend was a fellow baby Boomer and his comment was that he did not understand how the audience was paying attention to what the speaker had to say. The reality of the situation was that the majority of the Millennials in the audience were in fact engaged, but in a way that was different. They were sharing their experiences, and what they were learning, with their friends in real time by texting, tweeting and sending photos electronically.

Chris regularly experiences the same phenomena when he is watching a TV with his two daughters. Both are in their 20s and when they watch the TV, on their laps are a smart phone and a tablet on which they interact continuously. They are always connected and engaged with multiple friends at the same time they are watching a movie or TV.

What is the importance of the internet and social networking to the title industry? In the years to come, buyers and sellers will become the actual customers, and they will engage with a title company through the internet, or the technology that replaces the internet. The question becomes, how will you optimize your sales strategies and tactics for the changing landscape?

Brian Solis in his book, *What's The Future Of Business*[28] makes the case for three distinct customer segments in the digital age: the Traditional customer, the Digital customer, and the Connected customer. These three groups often separate along age parameters, but it is a mistake to use age as selection criteria.

The Traditional customer is typically represented by someone who has been in the business for a number of years, uses e-mail and a computer, but who chooses not to engage digitally

---

[28] Brian Solis, *What's The Future Of Business: Changing The Way Businesses Create Experiences.* (New Jersey: John Wiley & Sons, 2013).

with great frequency or perhaps does not have the acquired skill. In your 80\20 analyses of your current customer base, you will likely find many Traditional customers who have low digital acuity. This customer group obviously remains very important and the ways you communicate and interact with them will not change significantly.

The Digital customer segment represents a transitional group. These customers spend quite a bit of time on the internet, use one or two mobile devices, and are active in social or business networks like LinkedIn. These customers have good skills when it comes to digital acuity. In fact, for this group, their learning curve is active and they are choosing to use technology in its various forms at an increasing rate. This is an important group to consider because many will have been in the business for a number of years, are already quite successful, and the ways in which you engage with them will increasingly involve digital platforms and devices.

The third group, those who are connected, is represented primarily by the Millennials; those born between 1982 and 2004. They are connected all the time. For them, being connected is the way of life. They were handed a digital device to use at an early age and they have not looked back. Millennials think of themselves as belonging to a larger community of fellow digital users. They trust each other's opinions and recommendations shared electronically in a myriad of ways. They blog, they post their opinions freely on

Twitter and Facebook, they first look to the internet and their shared networks to research, comment, talk about something they like or don't like, and learn about anything and everything. Consumers who are connected digitally and are do-it-your-self-types are a growing customer segment who have materialized in the real estate market as For Sales By Owners (FSBO).

These customers turn to real estate platforms like Tulia and Zillow before they do anything else. They will find out online from other like-minded individuals where to go for resources to help in the home selling or buying process. They may search on Google to find out about local title agencies and services. Will your company name turn up first when they Google? When they click on your internet link, what will they find on your website that will help them know what steps to follow to sell or buy a home? Do you have an easy way for them to engage with you digitally? Will the experience on your website, or by using one of your Apps, be the same quality and type of experience as when they walk into one of your brick and mortar sites? After they use your escrow services, will they "like" you on your company's Facebook page resulting in their 200 or more connected friends seeing the praise? Will they write a review of the service they received so that you can post it on one of the networks your company advertises it uses?

It would be a mistake for us to recommend you embrace new digital technology, or a particular digital platform, network or

233

App just because it is in fashion. As we have repeatedly said throughout this book, it is important for you to understand what your customer's value.

In the digital age, this means knowing how they are behaving electronically, what their preferences are, and what are the best ways for you to engage with them. Throughout our consulting years, one concept we have used to discover customer preferences and ways title companies can better interact with customers is to identify critical points of customer contact. What Jan Carlson called Moments of Truth.[29]

We have studied critical points of customer contact or engagement by first examining workflow starting at the point of order entry and continuing all the way through to final policy production. This workflow approach maps out a path that is primarily linear in progression in terms of the points and types of contact the customer traditionally makes with a title company. Looking ahead, as more and more customers become connected digitally, the traditional points of contact will become more varied and less linear.

One customer may find your company through a Google search. Another customer may read a review or see an opinion

---

[29] Jan Carlson, *Moments of Truth*. (Harper Business; Reprint edition, 1989).

about your company on a social network. Another customer may find your name and contact information on an App supplied by a third party vendor. Still another potential customer may see a Tweet provided by someone they follow about a closing they just experienced. The types of methods and the timing and circumstances for how and when a customer chooses to engage with your company are changing and they will continue to be more numerous in the future.

The task for title companies is to design how customers can digitally engage with the company, what they will experience when they do, and how the experience is seamlessly integrated with the other systems and units of the company.

In designing this future system, the types of engagement you facilitate and promote should be functional for the customer and provide value. Here is a list of ideas to consider in planning for and designing how your company can engage with customers and customers can engage with you digitally, to increase sales:

1. Consider forming a design team to brainstorm the different ways customers can engage with you digitally going forward. Choose Millennials you have on your staff who are creative and think outside of the box. Challenge them to consider how to adapt to the business world what they do electronically in their private lives. Design your digital

framework to be consistent with your overall company values and vision.

2. Rethink the critical points of customer contact and the ways customers will engage with your company through a digital lens. Do not overlook the idea of contact before, during and after the traditional transaction process, but also include the other possible ways customers may engage electronically. Make your means of digital engagement integrated with each other and not stand-alone.

3. A big part of social networking is having something to talk about. Design routine ways to push information out to the customer to give the connected customer something to talk about.

4. If you have dedicated staff that operate a customer service unit, consider having them routinely mine business and social networks to discover information that may augment your engagement strategy.

5. Ask customers who are digitally connected to post a review of service after a closing.

6. Get customers to engage with your blog by asking them to provide you with ideas on how to improve service or products.

7. If your sales staff use and develop customer profiles, add a section to the profile that describes the customer's digital preferences.

8. Do not forget metrics. You need ways to evaluate your digital engagement strategies. Consider counting positive endorsements, reviews, referrals, Tweets about your company, references to your company on networks, subscribers to your blog, activity or responses on your blog, and clicks on your web pages, among other possible metrics. These metrics should be correlated with your traditional financial performance measures (i.e., increases in orders, revenue, etc.)

9. Farm networks like LinkedIn for leads.

10. Look ahead and consider how the role of the sales person will be changing for your company. Will more online orders and transactions mean that sales staff will be spending less face time with certain customers? What will their new roles be?

## GUIDING PRINCIPLES FOR CHAPTER 13

1.  Getting to the front of the real estate transaction channel is still a relevant and important strategy for sales but the new master at the head of the channel is the emerging connected (Wi-Fi) customer.

2.  The internet provides the opportunity for the customer to research, study, explore, compare, and reach decisions entirely on their own without gatekeepers, filters or go-betweens.

3.  By 2025, seventy-five percent of the workforce will be made up of Millennials, those born between the early 1980's and the early 2000's.

4.  In the years to come, the customer landscape will be changing along with the ways in which customers engage with your company and make buying decisions.

5.  Consumers who are connected digitally and who are do-it-your-self-types are a growing customer segment who have materialized in the real estate market as For Sales By Owners.

6.  In the Digital Age, understanding what customers value means knowing how they are behaving electronically, what their preferences are, and what are the best ways for you to engage with them.

## DEVELOPMENT IDEAS\QUESTIONS FOR CHAPTER 13

1.  Form a design team to study how customers currently engage with you electronically. Study your 80\20 analyses to help target which customers use digital platforms of some type. Brainstorm on ways to improve the different ways you engage digitally now, and will need to, in the future.

2.  Ask your customers for ideas on how to improve your connectivity.

3.  Develop an action plan to improve your digital connectivity and engagement.

# SELECTING A STRATEGY

## CHAPTER 14

In chapter 13 we emphasized that in the years to come, the customer landscape will be changing along with the ways in which customers choose to engage with a title insurance company. As you look ahead, the strategies and tactics you choose will have a significant impact on whether you succeed or grow your business, or become stagnant in the evolving marketplace. One important question is:

- How do I know which strategy or set of strategies will be the best for my company?

We worked with several agency owners whose strategy for growing revenue was acquiring title companies in countries where they did not have an office. One owner's strategy was growth by acquisition or startup. Meaning he would either buy an existing business or start a storefront and develop the business over time. These are similar strategies, but with very different operational and financial expectations. When he acquired an existing business he looked for a solid performer, perhaps with an older owner looking to get out, he paid over market value, and he tied the owner into a three to five year contract. In this type of acquisition, he paid for the revenue and he expected immediate results.

On the other hand, when he moved into a county or state with a startup he had less expense and he expected the startup to lose money for at least three years. Startups were managed differently and had different expectations.

Over time, his company expanded into adjoining states and internally he developed a group of advisors who became experts in acquisitions and startup. What is interesting about this story is even as successful as this group was, when they tried a new strategy like selling life insurance or homeowners insurance they were unsuccessful because they had no experience with other businesses. This company was best when it struck to what it knew, something recommended by Jim Collins.[30]

Collins in his book Good to Great talked about the Hedgehog Concept in which he provided examples of companies that focused on the one thing they did best and became great. The contrast is companies that act more like a Fox. They try to stay ahead of the pack and when they try to innovate or diversify, they sometimes fail.

We offer this example because we know another agency owner who is continually looking for new opportunities. He loves

---

[30] http://www.success.com/article/jim-collins-hedgehog-concept
http://www.jimcollins.com/article_topics/articles/good-to-great.html

new ideas and examining different and creative approaches. His employees would say that he is continually shaking the bushes to find new opportunities to pursue and change in his company is a way of life. This owner created a team that uses new ideas and innovation and are successful at both traditional strategies and new innovative ideas.

When it comes time to select a strategy or set of strategies for your company, you have to consider:

1.  Vision. Where do you see the company in five years?
2.  Goals. What are your goals?
3.  Hedgehog. What are you good at? What are your strengths? What expertise and experience do you have? What expertise or experience do you lack?
4.  What strategies fit with your vision, goals, and company?

The first consideration is whether you want to maintain your company as it exists today or become a different company in the future. You may be satisfied with continuing to run your company as it is until you either retire or sell. We have known quite a few owners who either have no desire to build their companies for the future or the capacity to do so. The problem is a business declines over time if it loses momentum in the marketplace or fails to change with the times.

243

The alternative path is developing and growing your company to be something you are not today. Neither of these paths are inherently right or wrong, but both demand that you make strategic choices. There are clear consequences for any strategic choice and the informed owner or leader should know what those implications are before deciding on one path over the other. Deciding to go into other lines of insurance when you know nothing about running such a business might sound exciting but it violates the Hedgehog Concept.

To help in your decision-making, we offer a few guidelines for making choices that fit with your overall company goals. You can use these guidelines to help you make critical decisions, or at more micro levels, to determine specific strategies and tactics to pursue for specific customer segments.

We recommend submitting your strategy ideas to a set of filters that will help determine their overall value to you. Think of these filters as a set of tests, each idea must pass through.

The first test (filter) for any strategy or pair of strategies is determining the cost and benefits of each potential strategy. A cost-benefit analysis (CBA) was first described by the French economist Jules Dupuit in 1848.[31] Basically the question you are asking is how does the cost and result of any strategy compare to simply investing

---

[31] http://en.wikipedia.org/wiki/Cost%E2%80%93benefit_analysis

the money. Over time, the cost-benefit analysis became a way to compare strategies using a nine-step process.[32]

The steps are:

1. List alternative projects/programs.
2. List stakeholders.
3. Select measurement(s) and measure all cost/benefit elements.
4. Predict outcome of cost and benefits over the relevant time period.
5. Convert all costs and benefits into a common currency.
6. Apply discount rate.
7. Calculate net present value of project options.
8. Perform sensitivity analysis.
9. Adopt recommended choice.

The first step is to identify alternatives, for example startup or acquisition. The second step is to identify the people involved in each strategy. In our experience, a strategy fails often because the people let it fail. Lack of leadership and resistance to change are the greatest barrier to any new strategy. The next step is to measure

---

[32]Anthony Boardman, David Greenberg, Aidan Vining, and David Weimer, Cost-Benefit Analysis (4th Edition) (The Pearson Series in Economics) [Paperback], Prentice Hall, 2010).

the cost and immediate benefit or loss for implementing each strategy. To determine the benefits you have to consider:

1. Effects on users or participants
2. Effects on non-users or non-participants
3. External (market) effects
4. Other social benefits

Next, you have to estimate the cost and benefit you will receive from each strategy over time. For example, in a year or three years. Benefits can be expressed using dollar values (e.g., projected new sales) but you can also consider other benefits that are more descriptive in nature. For example, goodwill or being first in a market.

Ultimately, the costs and benefits have to be converted into one currency and the resulting ratio of your projected cost dollars to results (i.e., benefit dollars) is called a cost-benefit ratio.

Notice that the next step in the process says to apply a discount rate. This is a step you may have to skip because there will be no easy way to come up with a value, but the idea is people value money that they receive today more than the money they get in the future. Therefore, strategies that take longer will be undervalued.

The next step is to determine the net present value (NPV) of each option. The NPV is the difference between the sums of discounted cash inflows and cash outflows. It will attempt to compare the present value of money today to the value of money earned in the future, taking inflation and returns into account.

In general, if the dollar value of the benefits exceeds your input costs (a ratio greater than 1) the value of your strategy is greater. If on the other hand the cost-benefit ratio is less than 1, the strategy is likely less favorable, at least at first glance.

Before selecting a strategy, one last step is to consider the probability that a strategy will be implemented correctly or fully and the likelihood that it will result in the benefits you estimate. This value will change the calculation for each strategy.

In examining strategies comparing costs to likely benefits we have to remember the old adage that sometimes you have to spend money to make money. Determining results using dollars is the bottom line, but in deciding on strategy, taking a longer view is often times important. For example, in the company we mentioned at the beginning that used acquisition and startups, they learned that a startup took longer to become profitable, but it usually had fewer employees and operational problems and when the cost of acquiring an existing business was taken into account, the startups often were as or more cost effective.

For some strategies, it may take one or more years before you realize the dollar benefits. In determining benefits, sometimes you will need to consider a longer view.

To simplify the nine-step process, we recommend using a graph to plot the relation between cost and benefit over time or to use a four-square grid to estimate or rate the relative cost and benefit of different strategies. The line graph is especially useful in determining the break-even point for a project.

The four-square method is not a full-fledged cost/benefit analysis, but it provides a simple way to compare strategies. In the four-square, the worst outcome is shown in the lower left quadrant, labeled number "1". The best outcome is shown in the upper right quadrant, labeled number "4".

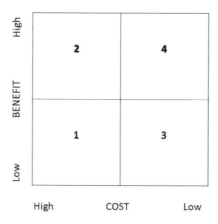

To select among different strategies using the four-square, method you start by estimating the costs to develop and implement each strategy in question including human costs. Next, for each strategy in question, consider the benefits or results implementing the strategy will produce after a fixed period of time. Consider benefits in dollars as well as operational results and other personnel and market effects.

Using the four quadrants of the grid on the previous page, position the strategies you are considering, according to their relative cost benefit comparisons. Along the vertical axis of the grid, benefits are considered from low to high. You have to use actual dollars for this scale. Along the horizontal axis of the grid, costs are considered this time from high to low. Cost and benefit have to be expressed in the same currency.

If the strategy you are considering is relatively high in cost and low in benefit it is plotted in Quadrant 1. If the strategy is low in benefit and low in cost, it belongs in Quadrant 3. If on the other hand, the strategy is low in cost and high in benefit, place the strategy in Quadrant 4.

Once you have all the strategies you are considering placed on the grid using the cost and benefit dimensions, you can systematically compare their relative value to help you decide which strategies merit further consideration.

In selecting strategies, a company's readiness to implement the strategy compared to the priority you have placed on it also should be considered. In other words, from an operations perspective, what is your immediate capability to implement a strategy compared to the importance or urgency of implementing that strategy? This is our second filter. Readiness is similar to the concept of sensitivity.

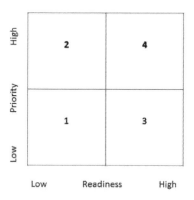

For example, consider that you want to develop an electronic application that customers can use on their smart phones or tablets to improve engagement with your company. You consider the costs for development, moderate but you also figure the future benefits in terms of customers placing orders and improved communications with your company are quite high. Your decision is that the strategy merits further consideration, so now you apply the readiness test. In doing so, you determine that your sales staff are technologically capable, have been repeatedly asking for the App development, and that the strategy has high priority because several competitors in your market place already have Apps of similar nature they are using with customers.

You use the grid in the same basic way, but this time you are not using dollars. Choose among the four quadrants based on your judgment of low and high readiness and low and high priority. In our example, your decision is that the readiness of your company is high for the App development and the strategy has high priority. You place the strategy in the upper right hand quadrant.

Here is a second example of the second filter. A sales strategy you are considering requires your sales staff to proportion a greater percentage of their time focusing on customers targeted for increased business opportunities. You figure the additional resources and time needed for implementation is low and the benefits will be high. Using the second grid, you determine that although your sales staff may be somewhat reluctant to re-proportion their time, the importance of increased sales and going after new business is paramount to your company. On the grid, you place this strategy as moderate in readiness, but very high in priority.

A third method to select strategies is designed for leaders who are primarily looking to grow and develop their companies.

251

The two variables on the grid are innovation and whether your strategy is aligned with the future of the company or title industry. In other words, where does your strategy fall on a continuum that considers creativity or innovation from low to high? Secondly, how well does the strategy line up with what the future of the title industry will look like in the years to come?

Granted, most of us are not futurists by profession. For years' people have been saying that lenders would take over the title industry, and that has not happened. Looking ahead to what the industry will be is more difficult than not. However, what we have said repeatedly is the title industry landscape is changing and a big part of it will increasingly rely on electronic innovations. There are other important variables regarding the future of the industry to consider as well. For example, the speed at which the industry is moving away from brick and mortar retail locations and relying more heavily on remote and electronic closings. We could write another book on these types of predictions, but perhaps the best judge in the end is what you believe in terms of the strategy you are considering. How do you rate whether the strategy you are considering is aligned with the future of the industry, low (i.e., not aligned or minimally aligned), or highly in line?

In some cases, whether you can predict the future of the industry may not matter as long as the strategy is in fact innovative. We can reliably say that if your strategy is not innovative or creative and it has not passed through our first two filters successfully, it is not worth considering any further.

On the third grid, first consider the relative strength of your strategy in terms of innovation. Is it innovative, new and creative or is it an accepted or more common practice already established in the market place? Next, consider how well your strategy matches up with the future of the industry. Does it align well with the future or will the strategy be out-of-synch with what the future holds?

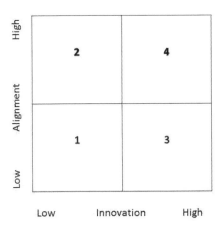

Consider our previous example of developing a mobile App. This strategy currently is being used already by many title companies. In terms of innovation, it is not very high on the scale, meaning it is not a new idea that will set you apart from many competitors. However, it does match up very well with the future

253

of the industry and would have to be rated high on that dimension. For that reason alone, it is a very important strategy to consider. We would place the strategy in Quadrant 2 on the third filter grid.

If you use the three pairs of decision filters: cost compared to benefit; readiness compared to priority; and innovation compared to alignment with the future, you will be in a better position to select a set of marketing and sales strategies for your company.

To make the process simpler, we developed a matrix of the six factors to derive a single score for each comparison and for an overall score. Consider the following example. Here we have a way to rate the cost and benefit on a 10-point scale.

| STRATEGY | | | | | | | | | | | | |
|----------|-----|---|---|---|---|---|---|---|---|------|-------|------|
| | Low | | | | | | | | | High | | |
| FACTORS | 1 | 2 | 3 | 4 | 5 | 6 | 7 | 8 | 9 | 10 | Score | Avg. |
| Cost | | | | | | | | | | | 0 | 0 |
| Benefit | | | | | | | | | | | 0 | |

From this we can derive a score for each factor and the average score for the two. Right away, you probably see a problem that we solved in the 2 X 2 grid by reversing the scale for Cost on the grid. Having a low cost should produce a higher rating.

This can be solved by reversing the scale for cost. For example, the lowest cost is a "10" and the highest cost is a "1". Once this problem is corrected mathematically, you can perform the three filter comparisons on the same matrix and easily compare two or more different strategies on each paired dimension or on total score.

In the following example, hiring a new sales person is compared to developing a new App. Each strategy scores the same on the cost/benefit comparison, a score of "4." This result makes additional comparisons useful. On the readiness / priority and innovation / alignment factors, developing the App show better results because the average score on each additional factor is higher and the overall score is higher.

| STRATEGY | | | | | | | | | | | | |
|---|---|---|---|---|---|---|---|---|---|---|---|---|
| Hire a Sales Person | Low | | | | | | | | | High | | |
| FACTORS | 1 | 2 | 3 | 4 | 5 | 6 | 7 | 8 | 9 | 10 | Score | Avg. |
| Cost | | | | | | | X | | | | 3 | 4 |
| Benefit | | | | | X | | | | | | 5 | |
| Readiness | X | | | | | | | | | | 1 | 3.5 |
| Priority | | | | | | X | | | | | 6 | |
| Innovation | | | | | X | | | | | | 5 | 4.5 |
| Alignment | | | | X | | | | | | | 4 | |
| | | | | | | | | | | | 24 | 4.00 |

| STRATEGY | | | | | | | | | | | | |
|---|---|---|---|---|---|---|---|---|---|---|---|---|
| Develop an App | Low | | | | | | | | | High | | |
| FACTORS | 1 | 2 | 3 | 4 | 5 | 6 | 7 | 8 | 9 | 10 | Score | Avg. |
| Cost* | | | | X | | | | | | | 6 | 4 |
| Benefit | | X | | | | | | | | | 2 | |
| Readiness | X | | | | | | X | | | | 8 | 6 |
| Priority | | | | X | | | | | | | 4 | |
| Innovation | | | X | | | | | | | | 3 | 5.5 |
| Alignment | | | | | | | | X | | | 8 | |
| | | | | | | | | | | | 31 | 5.17 |

Made in the USA
Middletown, DE
13 November 2014